ESSAYS IN
HISPANIC BIBLIOGRAPHY

ESSAYS IN
HISPANIC BIBLIOGRAPHY

by
Lawrence S. Thompson

THE SHOE STRING PRESS, INC.
1970

Publisher's Note

All but one of the following articles has been published previously. The material has been reset for this volume, but the style of original publication has been followed.

ISBN: 0-208-00978-7
Library of Congress Catalog Card Number: 75-96729
Printed in The United States Of America

TO MY MOTHER

Contents

Introduction

To the world of scholarship, L. S. Thompson needs no introduction. His work as a librarian, book reviewer, and scholar in fields that range from the Kentucky novel and folklore to the study of the history of book binding and printing is well known. His interest in Spanish American library and printing history goes back to the period between 1942 and 1945 when he served with the F.B.I. in Latin America. During this period he established enduring friendships with collectors, dealers, librarians and bibliographers. Much of the material in these essays stems from that experience. Subsequently he visited the Caribbean area, mainly Cuba (pre-Castro), Trinidad, Haiti and the Bahamas regularly and expanded his bibliological friendships. These essays reflect often the results of these travels.

Few librarians have Thompson's linguistic competence and it should immediately be noted that he has used this competence to provide the English-speaking reader with data concerning library and printing history which formerly has been available only in other languages, notably Spanish. His knowledge of research methods and of foreign languages has therefore opened new sources of information for the reader interested in the subjects of these essays.

"Resources for Research in Latin American Literature in Southern Libraries" is probably the first attempt to discuss and survey the important Latin American library collections in the South. Though it was written in 1953, most of this essay is still a valid description of at least the leading libraries in the field. Texas, Duke, Virginia, North Carolina, Florida, Florida State, Miami, Joint University libraries still possess the leading collections of the area. After almost two decades, they have continued to build in greater depth in their speciality. The scholar interested in library resources in Latin American literature will find this pioneering study in the field still a useful one. Without resorting to countless tables and statistics, he emphasizes the strengths of the several important library collections that he describes.

Extremely few scholars in the United States have been interested in Spanish American library history. Thompson's discussion of the libraries of colonial Spanish America is a valuable one not only for the information that it presents, but because it notes that this is a field which needs considerable more investigation. It has only been almost since the late 1930's that scholars have begun to destroy the black legend that claimed that libraries in Spanish America were insignificant. This brief study shows the widest knowledge of Spanish publications which deal with this subject. Individuals who do not read Spanish now have an excellent discussion of colonial Spanish American library history. Those who do read the language are provided with substantial leads through the numerous bibliographical citations found in the footnotes. This article has been translated and published in Spanish in a scholarly journal of Maracaibo, Venezuela. This is probably a good indication that such a succinct discussion of the subject did not exist in Spanish.

Dr. Thompson is well-acquainted with numerous library systems outside of the United States. His "Library Development in the English-Speaking West Indies" is based not only on pertinent publications concerning the area, but on several trips to this region. He speaks, therefore, from personal experience when he writes of the progress and library development in the West Indies. This article presents an excellent historical and descriptive study of library development along with suggestions on how library services and development could be improved

Almost twenty-five years ago, Thompson and Rivera Ruiz published their article on "The Libraries of Puerto Rico." A check with *Library Literature* shows that nothing has been written since this time in the English language concerning the history and general position of the libraries of this island commonwealth. This article remains then the chief source for knowledge in English on the libraries of Puerto Rico. The data found in it are based not only on retrospective publications in the Spanish language, but much of the information is based on important first-hand impressions. This article not only describes the history of libraries in Puerto Rico as well as the library situation of the early 1940s, but it makes recommendations concerning the future development of libraries in Puerto Rico.

The problem of bookbinding and its history has had a particular fascination for Dr. Thompson. Members of the library profession know of his rather gruesome account of the use of human skin in book binding. Yet, the account of early bindings in Spanish American books probably demanded just as much exacting research and scholarship as did the other study. Here too Thompson's discussion is unique in the English language. It too has been translated and published in Spanish, a sign, most likely, that the translation was viewed as filling a scholarly gap in knowledge of the subject. Thompson is able to use here his knowledge of bibliography, printing history and bookbinding in such a way as to provide the English-speaking individual with fresh and new insights into this problem.

There is little reason for me to discuss each of the essays. They have stood the test of time; the information they contain is still valid and useful. They are based on sound scholarly research and a thorough knowledge of what has already been written on the subject. Thompson has found subjects which have been little discussed in English and has developed this knowledge of Spanish American libraries, bibliography and printing history into a speciality that few other citizens of the United States are able to share with him.

It is fitting, therefore, that these essays should be brought together. In this way the student and scholar will not be forced to seek them out in their original journals and Festschriften.

I have learned from them, and it is my hope that others may profit from Thompson's knowledge as exemplified by these essays.

Hensley C. Woodbridge
Southern Illinois University

PART ONE

THE COLONIAL
PERIOD

The Libraries of Colonial Spanish America*

The *leyenda negra* has somehow perpetuated the idea that libraries were insignificant in colonial Spanish America, and this notion was a part of the folklore of Latin American history up until a quarter of a century ago. The stern legal prohibitions against the export of fiction to the Indies[1] and other formal controls on the book trade have been interpreted literally by some students who have not examined customs records, book lists in Jesuit and other religious archives, export records of the Casa de la Contratación (and countless other sources in the seemingly inexhaustible Archivo de Indias in Seville), Inquisition records, and other pertinent archives. The labors of scholars such as Irving A. Leonard,[2] José Torre Revello, and Father Guillermo Fúrlong Cárdiff,[3] using manuscript catalogues and book lists, have pointed out the productive sources for research; and their specialized studies have suggested the need for similar work in all fields of the history of the book in the old Spanish colonies. In particular we need to identify and describe more libraries that were in monasteries, episcopal palaces, universities, private homes, and, quite late in the colonial period, public institutions sponsored by societies.

Books came to the Americas at an early date. One of the first references to Bartolomé de las Casas (a Dominican) refers to a payment of 10,000 maravedís to the master of the vessel *Trinidad*

*Reprinted with permission of the publisher from *Biblioteca Docet: Festgabe für Carl Wehmer* (Amsterdam, Verlag der Erasmus—Buchhandlung, 1963), pp. 257-266.

for the passage of Las Casas „conn 4 criados, librería, ropa y media cámara"[4] on 6 April 1517. Seventeen years later and a whole hemisphere to the south the Franciscans entered the River Plata and brought books with them, and Pedro de Mendoza himself brought „siete libros medianos guarnecidos de cuero negro", one „librete chico dorado que dice que es Bridia guarnecido en pergamino".[5] Soldiers and administrators brought books to America, for they often had cultural interests in proportions equal to their desire for precious metals and *encomiendas.*

The friars—Jesuit, Dominican, Franciscan, Augustinian and Mercedarian—were the most zealous in bringing books to early Spanish America, much as the churchmen of early New England and New York, laid the foundations of the libraries of Harvard, Dartmouth, Yale and Columbia. Alonso de la Vera Cruz, an Augustinian distinguished as author, collector, and executive, came back to New Spain in 1573 with a scrap of the *lignum Crucis* and, vastly more important, a collection of books; and he founded and nurtured libraries in Mexico, Tiripitío, and Tacámbra. Some of his books are still preserved in the Museo Michoacana in Morelia.[6] Although we have not yet excavated records of significant libraries on the islands, we know that there was a collection in the Convento de Santo Domingo in San Juan de Puerto Rico as early as 1523 and that it endured until it was destroyed by the Dutch in 1625.[7] Lope de Vega even celebrated the private library of Bernardo de Valbuena, bishop of Puerto Rico from 1600 to 1627, in *Laurel de Apolo,* Silva II.

The Jesuits, more than any other order, were responsible for the spread of books and printing in Spanish America. Arriving in the Americas in the latter half of the sixteenth century, they brought with them not only the traditional vows but also concern for "a peculiar care in the education of boys". By the time of the expulsion in 1767, there were Jesuit libraries in Córdoba de Tucumán, Bogotá, and elsewhere which were at least equal to any in Saxon America. The dissolution was also the cause of the dispersal of Jesuit collections and their partial reincorporation into public and national libraries.[8] On the other hand, there were irreparable losses after the expulsion, and biblioklepts and biblioclasts had a Roman holiday in many an old cultural center such as Cuzco.

Jorge Cornejo Bouroncle found that the University of Cuzco, heir to the local Jesuit collections, was not able to inventory and to clean and repair the books until 1938;[9] and he was properly dismayed by a rumor, probably correct,[10] that a first edition of *Quijote* had been clandestinely removed from the library and sold.

If the surviving book lists in customs and Inquisition files, records of civil litigation, will books, and other likely sources were studied throughout Spanish America even to the extent they have been studied in Argentina, Chile, and Mexico, the rôle of Loyola's followers in developing book collections would be recognized as one of their greatest achievements. Especially in Argentina the Jesuits were active in creating libraries. Don Francisco Salcedo, dean of the Cathedral of Santiago del Estero and one of the first Jesuits to land in Argentina (around 1586) and Don Diego Suárez Babiano (d. 1593), vicar general of Córdoba, were masters of select, even if small private collections, and philology as well as theology was represented in the latter.[11] The Jesuits imported books steadily, both for library resources and for re-sale (mainly as textbooks) during the nearly two centuries from 1586 to 1767, when they were the dominant cultural element in the old viceroyalty of the Río de la Plata. Many personal libraries of individual friars found their way to the shelves of the old University of Córdoba, a trend which Father Fúrlong has documented. The Colegio Máximo and the Noviciado in Córdoba contained well over 5,000 volumes in 1767, and the Colegio Grande (or of San Ignacio) in Buenos Aires had upwards of 3,000 volumes. Many of the books in these two collections as well as in the provincial Jesuit libraries found their way to the modern University of Córdoba Library, to the Argentine National Library, and to other collections in the Buenos Aires and (in isolated instances) in the provinces.

In Santa Fé de Bogotá the Jesuit library of the Colegio de San Bartolomé was the cornerstone of the Biblioteca Pública, founded in 1774, barely seven years after the expulsion.[12] It was not actually opened to the public until 9 January 1777, at which time it consisted of 4,182 volumes, mainly in theology, history, and the classics.[13] This collection was the origin of the modern Columbian National Library.

In the opposite corner of the old kingdom of New Granada we can identify a founder of libraries in the brilliant *zambo* Francisco Javier Eugenio de Santa Cruz y Espejo (1747–1795) of Quito. A typical eighteenth century intellectual (and such there were in some abundance, in the Spanish colonies, the *leyenda negra* to the contrary), saw an opportunity to found a public library in the Ecuadorean capital from the remains of the Jesuit collections.[14] The especially harsh treatment of the Jesuits in Ecuador probably caused the destruction of many records, including library lists, and we may never know the full extent and importance of their collections.

In Santiago de Chile the Jesuit collections of some 5,000 volumes, were deposited in the University of San Felipe in Santiago where they remained almost unused. Largely theological and legal, with some classics,[15] this collection, and that of the University proper, amounting to some 8,000 volumes in all, became the nucleus of the Chilean National Library under the sponsorship of Manuel de Salas and San Martín. The significant fact, however, is that the Jesuits owned over 15,000 books in thirty-three different locations in Chile before 1767.

The brilliance of the Jesuits as missionaries in the orient and in the New World sometimes tends to obscure the work of the other orders. The Augustinians were pioneers in the transplantation of Hispanic culture, and Alonso de la Vera Cruz was among the first of many distinguished representatives of this order. Toward the end of the eighteenth century there were substantial libraries of at least four orders, in addition to the Jesuit collections, in Santiago de Chile. There were 5,000 volumes in the library of the Convento de Santo Domingo and 3,000 in the Convento de San Agustín.[16] The latter was based on a collection inherited from Fray Agustín Carrillo de Ojeda, who died in Lima in 1671, and a donation of 400 books by Fray Francisco de Loyola y Vergara in 1672. A manuscript catalogue in the Biblioteca Nacional of Santiago de Chile shows over 3,000 volumes in the Convento de San Francisco in that city. Even the Mercedarians, rarely distinguished as book-lovers or scholars, had 435 books in their Convento de La Merced when it was founded in 1683; and a century later there were about 1,000 volumes in the collection.[17]

In Buenos Aires the Dominicans had a library of at least a thousand titles in 1739 when the Dominican Neìra referred to it in complimentary terms.[18] In 1768 the bishop of Buenos Aires wrote to Count de Aranda that the Dominican monasteries, as well as those of other orders, in his province, were poorly equipped with books,[19] but this was probably a hint to have Jesuit property turned over to them. There were Dominican, Franciscan and Mercedarian libraries in the Río de la Plata, and it is not unusual to find books in modern Argentine libraries, public and private, with such inscriptions as "Es de la Merced de Córdoba". The detailed study of these collections awaits the excavation of more catalogues from archival sources.

The Franciscans were second only to the Jesuits in bold and imaginative missionary work in which books played a major rôle. The first library in what is now the United States was the Franciscan collection in Santa Fé, New Mexico, and it may have come into existence three decades before John Harvard's legacy reached Cambridge, Massachusetts. While the local Franciscan archives perished along with those of the provincial government in the Pueblo Revolt of 1680, Eleanor B. Adams and France V. Scholes have made logical guesses about the scope and content of the collection, mainly from letters written by Fray Juan de Vidania around 1640/41 at the time of a bitter controversy between Governor Luís de Rosas and the Franciscans.[20] Vidania cited many authorities, mainly religious, but also classical, and it is likely that the original sources were at hand.

The Franciscans in the capital were reputed to have developed the best book collection in Mexico. Fernando Peñalosa states, without citing documentation, that the friars of the Convento de San Francisco in Mexico City "spared neither expense nor effort in bringing together a great collection of books, and by the end of the eighteenth century they had the best library in New Spain".[21]

There are several known instances, and probably many other yet unrecorded ones, of high prelates who were book collectors and founders of libraries. Juan de Zumárraga, first bishop and archbishop of Mexico, and an indefatigable friend of printing, education, and cultural development in general, was a zealous collector and donated books to various monasteries.[22] In a report to the

Council of the Indies in 1533 he emphasized the need for good libraries in New Spain. Another early book-loving bishop of Mexico was Vasco de Quiroga, who became the first bishop of Michoacán in 1537.[23] His library of over 600 volumes must have been semi-public, for a humanitarian of his orientation would not fail to share his books as a part of his efforts to create a utopian society among the aborigines. Most famous of the bibliophilic Mexican prelates was Juan de Palafox y Mendoza.[24] An enemy of the privileged regular clergy (especially the Jesuits) and a humanitarian comparable to Las Casas, Palafox founded a seminary in Puebla, the Colegio de San Pedro y San Pablo, in 1646 and donated a library of 6,000 volumes. The institution thrived under Palafox' successors, and the library continues to be housed in a late eighteenth century building known as the Biblioteca Palafoxiana.

At the other extremity of Spanish America another private episcopal library survives in the Cabildo Eclesiástico of Santiago de Chile.[25] It originally belonged to Francisco Ruiz de Berecedo, born in Concepción in 1675. According to the Archivo de Escribanos, a rich source for documents relative to books in colonial Chile, the collection amounted to "2,058 libros grandes y pequeños, con sus estantes con 90 cajones". Strong in classical literature, history, and linguistics, the library passed to Berecedo's great nephew, Manuel de Alday y Axpée, later bishop of Santiago. He in turn left it to the Cathedral of Santiago.

In the latter part of the eighteenth century the Archbishop of Bogotá and Viceroy of New Granada, Antonio Caballero y Góngora, had a distinguished private collection.[26] He provided a subsidy for José Celestino Mutis in 1783 to establish the famous Expedición Botánica; and it is not unreasonable to assume that such a generous patron of science would make his library freely available to the beneficiaries of his grants.

We know less about the university libraries of colonial Spanish America than about libraries of the religious or of private individuals. Córdoba is the single exception to this statement, although it not unlikely that documents will some day be found to shed more light on colonial academic libraries. The early library history of the Imperial and Pontifical University of Santo Domingo, founded ninety-eight years before Harvard opened its doors, is unrecorded in print. The second oldest university of the New World in Mexico (1551) had existed for two and a half centuries when the Viceroy Marquina reported to his successor that the university "no tiene gabinete y su biblioteca está escasa de buenas obras modernas".[27] The University of Havana (1728) had a library from the beginning which served both the institution and the religious establishment with which it was affiliated. The university was under the direction of the clergy and remained so until the secularization in 1842, at which time an assistant professor in the Faculty of Philosophy and Letters was placed in charge.[28]

The seminaries could hold university rank and privilege and perform university functions (with libraries as a necessary tool). Good examples were the Colegio de San Bartolomé (Jesuit, *supra*) in Bogotá and the Colegio del Rosario (Dominican) in Bogotá, both equal in privileges to the University of Salamanca by royal decree; and their libraries were, according to Giraldo Jaramillo,[29] "famosas en la Santafé colonial". The Seminary of Santiago de Chile, founded in 1777, had five sections (*estantes*) of books, but we do not know how many volumes there were.[30] Palafox' solicitude for the library needs of his Colegio de San Pedro y San Pablo has already been noted.

Perhaps a contrast with North American colonial libraries is not out of order.[31] John Harvard willed his library of some 400 books in 1638 to the two-year-old-college in Cambridge, and the books passed to the exclusive control of the institution. In 1764 when Harvard Hall burned there were 5,000 volumes, but by 1790 the 404 surviving books had been increased to a total of 13,000. A group of clergymen in Branford, Connecticut, assembled forty folio volumes for the new Collegiate School of Connecticut, and there were nearly 1,000 when they were moved to New Haven in 1716. The school acquired its present name when Elihu Yale gave 400 volumes in 1720. In 1733 Bishop Berkeley gave 100 more books. By 1765 there were 4,000 volumes under the supervision of the college's administration. Princeton University owned some 3,000 volumes in 1802 when Nassau Hall burned, and Dartmouth College held 3,000 books by 1809. The significant fact about these and other colleges (in the Anglo-American sense) is that the clergy was not the final determinative force in the institution's destinies. Administration of the book collections was no more efficient, perhaps less efficient in some instances, and the collections in Cambridge and New Haven may even have been inferior to those of Córdoba, Bogotá, Mexico City, or Santiago de Chile. But the Calvinist and Anglican clergy did not rise and fall with the political destinies of the country; and, while they dominated the teaching faculties, the institutions had powerful friends outside of the clergy. The Roman church performed fabulous exploits in bringing culture to the New World, but there was far too intimate a connection between church and state to insure stability for the other partner when one had problems. A débacle such as the Jesuit expulsion had disastrous effects on all institutions associated with this group.

There is another side of the picture towards the end of the colonial period that was manifest from Cambridge to Córdoba: the influence of the Enlightenment. The propagation of secular libraries and freedom of learning was a fundamental notion of the new movement, and in Spanish America we even find the clergy (by no means totally reactionary) participating in the movement. The same spirit that moved Benjamin Franklin and his friends to establish the Library Company of Philadelphia and what is today the University of Pennsylvania was also abroad from New Orleans to Buenos Aires. If these libraries and universities did not thrive in nineteenth-century Spanish America, penetration of the ideas of the Enlightenment to the old Spanish colonies is nevertheless beyond question.[32]

If some of the Jesuit persecution (especially in the Americas) was tinged with jealousy and vengefulness, it was surely a more generous attitude that inspired the conversion of old Jesuit collections to the use of semi-public, university, and later national libraries. This we have already noted in Quito, Bogotá, Córdoba and Buenos Aires, where substantial portions of Jesuit collections escaped the biblioklepts and biblioclasts to find their way to semi-public collections. The clergy often encouraged the establishment of a "public" library (actually not quite public in the nineteenth century Anglo-American sense) and made substantial donations of books for the purpose.[33] In 1788 the Cathedral of Mexico accepted and opened for public use the Biblioteca Turriana, founded by the two brothers Torres, and their uncle.[34] The municipal government of Mexico City made contributions to its support, and it is said to have accumulated 19,000 volumes.

Perhaps the most characteristic manifestation of the spirit of the Enlightenment as far as Spanish American library development is concerned is the Sociedad Económica de Amigos del País in Havana. Founded by several Havana gentlemen, to "aumentar la instrucción y de influir el gusto de la lectura",[35] it was to be financed by funds derived from the sale of the *Papel periódico*. The serial itself commenced in 1790 and was produced by the Imprenta de la Capitanía General. Members of the Sociedad Económica contributed books, and there was an ambitious plan to exchange with other Hispanic countries. It is doubtful that this plan was ever realized, even in part, for world political conditions and the current system of communications were hardly conducive to international cooperation at this time. It is significant to note that this institution, essentially a subscription library for the intellectual élite of the Cuban capital, thrived for another century of colonial administration and more than a half century of the first Cuban republic. In the late 1950s it was still the most practical collection in Havana for researchers in things Cuban.

Manuel del Socorro Rodríguez, a Cuban émigré to New Granada, also combined journalism and librarianship. On 9 February 1791 he published the first number of the *Papel periódico de la ciudad de Santafé de Bogotá* and continued it until 6 January 1797. In the meanwhile he catalogued both the printed books and manuscripts in the "Real Biblioteca Pública" and, presumably, made them much more accessible than at any previous time.[36] Even if the libraries in Bogotá and Buenos Aires were precursors of actual revolution, the same spirit of rational truth-seeking nevertheless inspired these as well as the founders of the library of the Sociedad Económica in Havana, where revolution was not to be successful for another century.

Another element in the growth of libraries for laymen in the late eighteenth century was the rising economic prosperity of Spanish America. In 1802 Pedro de Mantilla, resident agent in Madrid for the Consulado (merchant guild) of Mexico, presented a list of "recognized works in political economy" which seemed appropriate for a library for the Consulado in Veracruz. There is no evidence that the library ever actually came into existence, but the list, published by Irving A. Leonard and Robert S. Smith,[37] reveals something of the growing awareness of businessmen of the need for reference books.

The *leyenda negra* can be transformed into a smog-yellow by careful study of the zeal of intellectuals, clerical and secular, in the Spanish colonies just before the revolutions. Indeed, there was never any Plutonian darkness, from the days of Las Casas on. The witchcraft scandals of New England and the anti-intellectualism of Virginia's seventeenth century governors might have been the basis of a similar malignancy by enemies of the English colonial administration; but, instead, Saxon America has been apotheosized (mainly by North American writers) as a cradle of modern egalitarianism. In Spanish America there are records of savage action against owners of private libraries including books not fully approved by the ecclesiastical hierarchy, but there are also numerous instances of private ownership of books which would have been vigorously condemned by orthodox Philadelphia Quakers or tidewater Anglicans. The truth of the matter is, probably, that possession of questionable books was used as an excuse by authorities for action against politically suspect individuals. The records of private libraries, abundant in lay and clerical circles alike, are known in representative samples, thanks to the work of Rodríguez Marín, Torre Revello, Leonard, O'Gorman,[38] González Obregón,[39] Fúrlong, and other delvers in the archives of two hemispheres.

The story of private bibliophily in colonial Spanish America is beyond the scope of this essay, but it cannot be ignored in this connection; for private collections have always set the tone for the public collections into which they have been incorporated or to which they are often dispersed. Religious books predominated, but we have seen that the "lying histories" found their way to the Indies despite legal prohibitions. One of Pedro de Mendoza's books was by Erasmus.[40] It might even be a bit impious to try to guess what titles were among the two hundred books brought by Antonio de Mendoza, first viceroy of New Spain, for his entertainment in his new post. He was cautious to arrange to have them exempted from customary duties—and presumably inspection as well—by special dispensation of the Crown.[41]

There were regrettable cases of persecution. Saddest of those recorded is the fate of Melchór Pérez de Soto, who was arrested on 10 January 1655 in his Mexico City residence and died two months later in a secret prison of the Holy Office.[42] He had "1502 cuerpos de libros. . . . en latín y en romance" (and, *horribile dictu*, in High and Low Dutch, presumably Lutheran in content). He had books in bibliography (León Pinelo's *Epitome*), the sciences (Copernicus and Euclid), Mexican imprints, and French sonnets. The existing records fail to show what the Holy Office had against Pérez de Soto in addition to being the master of a library of a typical seventeenth century cultured layman. There must have been more to the story. In remote Santa Fé de Nueva México the Holy Office arrested Bernardo López de Mendizabal and his wife Doña Teresa in 1662; and the inventory of their books showed such subversive titles as *Quijote*, a book of *comedias* by different authors, *Orlando Furioso*, and Espinel's *Marcos de Obregón*.[43] By the same token, Diego de Peñalosa, successor of Luís de Rosas as governor of New Mexico, ran afoul of the Church. He was arrested and his books and property inventoried in 1665. Far to the south of Mexico, Francisco de Larrinaga, bibliophilic *corregidor* in Mendoza in the late seventeenth century, was staked out in the desert by his cruel successor, Nicolás Francisco de Retana, but fortunately was rescued by passing Indians. Retana seems not to have bothered to have indicted Larrinaga for the ownership of some seventy volumes of mathematics, architecture, law and theology,[44] some of which may well have been by Lutheran authors.

There were, in fact, an abundance of dissident and even heretical books in Spanish American libraries toward the end of the eighteenth century. Manuel Gayoso de Lemos, governor of Louisiana from 1797 until his death in 1799, could get away with ownership of any books he wanted to read, including William Robertson's notoriously anti-Spanish *History of America*.[45] In the Río de la Plata apparently little attention was paid by the end of the eighteenth century to formal prohibitions against importation or possession of questionable books. Ricardo R. Caillet-Bois notes in various private collections the *Encyclopédie,* works of Voltaire, Bayle, Montesquieu and even the Abbé Raynal (a founding father of the *leyenda negra*).[46].

Even in colonial Caracas, a city ranking below Bogotá in cultural importance for New Granada, the young Bolívar could read Locke, Condillac, Buffon, d'Alembert, Helvetius, Montesquieu, Lalande, Rousseau, Voltaire, Rollin, Berthel, and the principal ancient and modern belletristic authors, philosophers, historians, and poets of western Europe, including England.[47] Many another youngster who participated actively in fomenting and executing the revolutions of the early nineteenth century must have had a similar background.

Whether all of these books which were surely suspect to officials in Spain were also available in institutional or religious libraries is not known. If they were in the latter, they were surely available only to a select few. The doubt in our minds that is left by the absence of published lists and more detailed histories of institutional libraries suggests the urgent need for more investigations of the type that Leonard and other students with similar interests have made on private libraries and the book trade. Many original archives have been lost, but many others survive and need only to be located, transcribed, and interpreted. Until they are, our imperfect knowledge of the institutional libraries of colonial Spanish America will remain one of our greatest handicaps in adequate understanding of three centuries of American history.

NOTES

1. Real cédula issued in Ocaña, 4 April 1531. See also the legal code for the Indies, the *Recopilación de leyes de Indias* (Madrid, A. Balbas, 1756; 4 vols.), especially Ley 4, Título 24, Libro I, for laws governing books. Control of the flow of books to the Indies (by the Casa de la Contratación in Old Spain and by customs agents in the New World) is best summarized by José Torre Revello, *El libro, la imprenta y el periodismo en América durante la dominación española* (Buenos Aires, 1940; Universidad de Buenos Aires, Facultad de Filosofía y Letras, Instituto de Investigaciones Históricas, „Publicaciones", LXXIV), pp. 37-93; but we need a definitive study based on additional source material before we can understand properly the rôle of books in the Spanish colonies.

2. Leonard's years of research in archival depositories in Seville, Mexico City, Lima, Bogotá, Santiago de Chile, and Buenos Aires were ably summarized in his *Books of the Brave, Being an Account of Books and of Men in the Spanish Conquest and Settlement of the Sixteenth Century New World* (Cambridge, Mass., Harvard University Press, 1949).

3. „Las bibliotecas coloniales en el Río de la Plata", *Boletín de la Academia Nacional de la Historia,* XIII (1940), 115-148, and *Bibliotecas Argentinas durante la dominación Española* (Buenos Aires, Editorial Huarpes, 1944; „Cultura colonial Argentina", 1).

4. Archivo General de las Indias, Contratación 4675, cuadernos, p. 83, vuelta, *apud* Lewis Hanke and Manuel Giménez Fernández, *Bartolomé de las Casas, 1474-1566, bibliografía crítica y cuerpo de materiales para el estudio de su vida, Escritos, actuación y polémicas que suscitaron durante cuatro siglos* (Santiago de Chile, Fondo Histórico y Bibliográfica, José Toribio Medina, 1954), p. 8.

5. Enrique A. Peña, ed., *Documentos relativos a la expedición de D. Pedro de Mendoza y aconteci ocurridos en Buenos Aires desde 1536 a 1541* (Buenos Aires, Imprenta Angel Curtola, 1936), p. 245.

6. Amancio Bolaño e Isla, *Contribución al estudio bibliográfico de fray Alonso de la Vera Cruz,* prólogo de Augustín Millares Carlo (Mexico, Robredo, 1947; „Biblioteca histórica mexicana de obras inéditas", 21), pagina 24, and Joaquín García Icazbalceta, *Bibliografía mexicana del siglo XVI,* nueva edición por Augustín Millares Carlo (México, Fondo de Cultura Económica, 1954), p. 147. A contemporary witness of Fray Alonso's zeal as a founder of libraries is Jerónimo Román in his *Republicas del mundo* (Salamanca, 1594-1595). „Republica christiana", liber XV, cap. 15 (incorrectly numbered 17). See also Felipe Teixido, *Ex libris y bibliotecas de Mexico* (Mexico, Secretaría de Relaciones Exteriores, 1939; „Monografías bibliográficas mexicanas", 20).

7. Lawrence S. Thompson and Jorge Rivera Ruiz, „The Libraries of Puerto Rico", *Library Quarterly,* XVI (1946,) 225.

8. See sections on Colombia and Argentina, in Gerald Herbert Sandy, *An Account of the National Libraries of Spanish South America* (Urbana, Illinois, 1932; typewritten M.A.L.S. thesis). A classic case of dispersion (in which, as the author aptly quotes Holy Writ, „ et super vestem . . . miserunt sortem") is recorded by Pablo Cabrera, „La antigua biblioteca jesuítica de Córdoba", *Revista de la Universidad Nacional de Córdoba,* XVII (1930), 175-216.

9. „Libros antiguos", in *Proceedings of the Third Convention of the Inter-American Bibliographical and Library Association,* Washington, D.C., February 23 and 24, 1940 (New York, H. W. Wilson, 1941; Inter-American Bibliographical and Library Association, *Publication,* Series II, vol. 3), pp. 83-85.

10. Probably correct, for it is not unlikely that the entire first edition was shipped to America. See Francisco Rodríguez Marín, *El „Quijote" y Don Quijote en América* (Madrid, Librería de los sucesores de Hernando, 1911); Leonard, *op. cit.,* p. 270; and Leonard, *Romances of Chivalry in the Spanish Indies, with Some Registros of Shipments of Books to the Spanish Colonies*

(Berkeley, University of California Press, 1933; "University of California Publications in Modern Philology", vol. 16, no. 3).

11. Fúrlong, „Las bibliotecas coloniales", p. 121.

12. Gabriel Giraldo Jaramillo *et al.*, *Incunables bogotanos; siglo XVIII* (Bogotá, Banco de la República, Biblioteca „Luís-Angel Arango", 1959), p. 8. In this introductory essay on „El libro y la imprenta en la cultura colombiana" Giraldo Jaramillo refers to the library of the Colegio del Rosario as the other famous collection of colonial Santa Fé de Bogotá.

13. *El Diario Nacional* (Bogotá), 20 February 1919.

14. Clarence Henry Haring, *The Spanish Empire in America* (New York, Oxford University Press, 1947), p. 240. See also Richard Pattee, „Libraries and Archives for Historical Research in Ecuador", *Hispanic American Historical Review*, XVII (1937), 234.

15. Chile, Oficina Central de Estadística, *Anuario estadístico* (Santiago, 1909), p. 504. Tomás Thayer Ojeda, „Las bibliotecas coloniales de Chile", *Revista de bibliografía chilena y extranjera*, I (pt.i, 1913), 34-36, 86-87, 149-151 219-221, and I (pt. ii, 1913), 4-7, 73-76 „La biblioteca de un médico a principios del siglo XVII", by E. Vaïsse, 141-144, 189-194, 253-255, has examined the Jesuit archives of this jurisdiction and reported 6,000 books in the Colegio de San Miguel at the time of the expulsion.

16. J.I.V. Eyzaguirre, *Historia eclesiástica, política y literaria de Chile* (Valparaiso, Impr. del Comercio, 1850; 3 vol.), II, 272.

17. Thayer Ojeda, *op cit.*, I, i ,150, and I, ii, 6, according to the records of this monastery, which, happily, have been preserved.

18. Fúrlong, „Las bibliotecas coloniales", *loc. cit.*, p. 130-131.

19. *Ibid.*, p. 140.

20. „Books in New Mexico, 1598-1680", *New Mexico Historical Review*, XVII (1942), 226-270.

21. „The Development of Libraries in Mexico", *Library Quarterly*, XXIII (1953), 116.

22. *Ibid.*, p. 115.

23. Silvio Zavala, *Ideario de Vasco de Quiroga* (Mexico, El Colegio de Mexico, 1941); *id., La „Utopia" de Thomás More in la Nueva España* (Mexico, Robredo, 1937; „Biblioteca mexicana de obras ineditas", 4); and Haring, *op. cit.*, p. 193.

24. Antonio Gonizález de Rosende, *Vida i virtudes del señor D. Juan de Palafox y Mendoza* (Madrid, J. de Paredes, 1666), and Hubert Howe Bancroft, *History of Mexico: Vol. III, 1600-1803* (San Francisco, A. L. Bancroft, 1883), pp. 112-113.

25. Thayer Ojeda, *op. cit.* I, ii, 253-254.

26. Giraldo Jaramillo, *op cit.*, p. 8.

27. „Instrucción del Señor Félix Berenguer de Marquina al Señor Iturrigaray", 1 January 1803, in *Instrucciones que los virreyes de Nueva España dejaron a sus sucesores* (Mexico, 1867-1873; 2 vols.), II, 629. It is doubtful that much more could be said about the venerable Universidad de San Marcos in

Lima, to judge from the paucity of information about books in the University in Luís Antonio Eguiguren, *La Universidad en el siglo XVI* (Lima, Imprenta Santa María,, 1951: Universidad Nacional Mayor de San Marcos, Publicaciones del cuarto centenario, „Historia de la Universidad", t. I, vol. I „narración").

28. Josefina Mayol and Jerrold Orne, „Cuban Libraries", *Library Quarterly*, XXII (1952), 92-124.

29. *Op. cit. p. 8.*

30. Thayer Ojedo, I, ii, 7.

31. See Albert Predeek and Lawrence S. Thompson, „Die Vereinigten Staaten von Nordamerika", in Georg Leyh, ed., *Handbuch der Bibliothekswissenschaft*, 3. Band, „Geschichte der Bibliotheken" (Wiesbaden, Harrassowitz, 1955), pp. 774-855. In the same volume Joris Vorstius has a note on colonial Spanish American libraries in his essay captioned „Die übrigen Kulturländer", p. 917, which reveals both the poverty of printed sources on Spanish American colonial library history (in sharp contrast with the material available to Predeek and Thompson) and Vorstius' own insight into the essential problems of the subject.

32. A. P. Whitaker, ed., *Latin America and the Enlightenment* (New York, Appleton, 1942).

33. Augustín Piaggio, *Influencia del clero en le independencia Argentina (1819-1820)* (Barcelona, Luis Gili, 1912), pp. 175-194. See also David Rubio, „Public Education, Books, and Libraries in Colonial South America", *Catholic Library World*, XI (1940), 99-110, an article in which factual coverage falls somewhat short of the ambitious title.

34. Peñalosa, *op. cit.*, p. 118.

35. *Actos de la Sociedad Económica de Amigos del País* (from the meeting of 30 May 1793), *apud* Mayol and Orne, *op. cit.*, p. 95. Due to current political conditions, it has not been possible to review these records in 1961. See also José Toribio Medina, *La imprenta en La Habana 1707-1810; notas bibliográficas* (Santiago de Chile, Imprenta Elzeviriana, 1704), p. XXVII *et seq.*, and p. 70 *et seq.* For a comparable society in colonial Puerto Rico see Thompson and Rivera Ruiz, *op. cit.*, p. 227.

36. Giraldo Jaramillo, *op. cit.*, pp. 12-13, and Joaquín Acosta, *Compendio histórica del descubrimiento y colonización de la Nueva Granada en el siglo décimo sexto* (Paris, Impr. de Beau, 1848).

37. „A Proposed Library for the Merchant Guild of Verazcruz, 1801", *Hispanic American Historical Review*, XXIV (1944), 84-102.

38. Edmundo O'Gorman, „Bibliotecas y librerías coloniales, 1585-1694", *Boletín del Archivo General de la Nación* México, X (1939), 661-1006.

39. Luis Gonzalez Obregón, *Libros y libreros en el siglo XVI* (Mexico, 1914; „Publicaciónes del Archivo General de la Nación", VI).

40. José Torre Revello, *La fundación y despoblación de Buenos Aires (1536-1541)* (Buenos Aires, Librería „Cervantes", J. Suárez, 1937), p. 87.

41. Ciriaco Pérez Bustamente, *Don Antonio de Mendoza, primer virrey de la Nueva España*, 1555-1550 (Santiago de Compostela, 1928; „Anales de la

Universidad de Santiago", III), p. 20 and appendix, document no. IV.

42. Manuel Romero de Terreros y Vinent (Marqués de San Francisco), *Un bibliófilo en el Santo Oficio* (Mexico, 1920), based on Inquisition records in the Archivo Nacional, a still unexhausted mine of information on books in New Spain.

43. Adams and Scholes, *op. cit.*, pp. 239-243.

44. Thayer Ojeda, *op. cit.*, I, ii, 254-255.

45. Irving A. Leonard, „A Frontier Library, 1799", *Hispanic American Historical Review*, XXIII (1943), 30.

46. *Ensayo sobre el Rio de la Plata y la Revolución francesa* (Buenos Aires, Imprenta de la Universidad, 1929; Buenos Aires, Universidad, Facultad de Filosofía y Letras, Instituto de Investigaciones Históricas, Publication Núm. 49), pp. 19-25.

47. Angel Grisanti, *La instrucción pública en Venezuela; época colonial; la independencia, y primeros años de la república época actual* (Barcelona, Araluce, 1933).

Book Illustration in
Colonial Spanish America [*]

If we accept Francisco Vindel's vigorous contention that the first book printed in America was *El Rezo del Santo Rosario*, Mexico, 1532-34, book illustration was a primary tool for the first American printer. A series of crude wood engravings appears on each leaf, for the book was clearly designed to teach the prayers of the Rosary to a humble and unlearned audience. I prefer to think that this audience was a European one of mid-century, rather than a Mexican one of 1532-34. Fortunately, or unfortunately, as the case may be, we have no example of the work of Esteban Martín, another alleged Mexican prototypographer, to plague us with probably insoluble problems of typography and illustration.

Even without the alleged priority of *El Rezo del Santo Rosario*, Mexico City was the first center of book production in the Americas and remained the most productive one from the colonial period to the present day. The tradition of decorating the printed page began early. Juan Pablos, generally unimaginative in his notions of typographical design, soon realized that there ought to be some decorative features to make his books more attractive, both to indigenous readers and to the flamboyant conquistador. Thus the title page of the *Doctrina Breve muy provechosa de las Cosas que Pertenecen a la Fe Catholica...*, 1543, has a xylographic border of a half-dozen different pieces arranged at random. The

*Reprinted with permission of the publisher from *Papers Presented at the Third Rare Book Conference of the American Library Association in 1962*, edited by Frances J. Brewer (Berlin, Gebr. Mann Verlag, 1963), pp. 22-34.

title, wood engraved on a solid block rather than set typographically, is surrounded by episcopal insignia (hat and tassels), repeatedly used on Mexican title pages throughout the century.

In 1544, the year following the publication of the *Doctrina Breve*, Pablos brought out an edition of Johannes Gerson's *Tripartito*, the first book printed in America that was illustrated with a full page wood engraving. The verso of the title page shows the Virgin presenting the chasuble to Saint Ildefonso, an attractive design, probably of Iberian origin. It was considered good enough by a later printer, Pedro Ocharte, for use in the *Doctrina Christiana en la Lengua Guasteca, cõ la Lengua Castellana*, 1571. Pablos had a few other woodcuts at his disposal, notably a fabulous Spanish royal armorial device which he used on the title page of the *Ordenanças y Copilaçión de Leyes*, 1548. In his edition of Fray Alonso de la Vera Cruz's *Recognitio Summularum*, 1554, Pablos introduced a wood engraving of Saint Augustine, also repeated by Ocharte in the *Doctrina Christiana en Lengua Guasteca*, and by Pablos himself in his *Constitutiones Fratrum Haeremitarum*, 1556. In Pablo's edition of Fray Alonso de Molina's *Vocabulario en la Lengua Castellana y Mexicano*, 1555, the stigmata of Saint Francis of Assisi appears on the title page, one of the most frequently repeated illustrations in sixteenth century Mexico. Pablos began to import more and more woodcuts in the latter part of his printing career, but he never developed a superior sense for book design. The fantastic dissections and rearrangements of his handful of woodcut borders demonstrate clearly his lack of originality in this area.

Most characteristic of the fortuitous selection of illustrations and of the fact that they were regarded and used as common property by all printers, is the title page of Fray Alonso de la Vera Cruz's edition of the *Dialectica Resolutio cum textu Aristotelis* printed by Pablos in 1554. The elaborate border with cherubs, warriors, a hippogryph, and a lion rampant—inter alia—is virtually identical with that used by Edward Whitchurch in London for his *Booke of the Common Prayer . . .* (for Edward VI) in 1549. Lucy Osborne studied the design and its history and published a detailed analysis in *The Library*, December, 1927.

Both Antonio de Espinosa and Pedro Ocharte, the second and

third printers of Mexico, were superior to Pablos in book design, but the scarcity of original woodcuts in the Americas caused them to depend heavily on the existing stock, augmented only gradually by imports.

Espinosa's skill as a designer and his tasteful use of illustrations are effectively brought out by Alexander A. M. Stols in his *Antonio de Espinosa, el Segundo Impresor Mexicano*, 1962. The thirty-five plates in Stols' book were carefully selected and offer abundant evidence for Espinosa's sophisticated tastes.

The origin of a domestic craft of wood engraving is shrouded in mystery. J. García Icazbalceta believes that the *Tumulo Imperial de la Gran Ciudad de Mexico,* Mexico, Antonio de Espinosa, 1560, contains an engraving of the imperial sepulcher of Charles V made in Mexico. He argues that the very short period of time that elapsed between the observance of the exequies and the printing of the book did not permit the engraving to be ordered from Spain. However, he does not allow for the possibility that the cut may have been sent, along with instructions to observe the solemnities, and to print a memorial of them.

Lawrence C. Wroth has told a better documented story of Fray Pedro Ortiz, who may have been Mexico's first illustrator and was surely the first one we know by name. According to Wroth's account in *The Colophon,* 1932, Ortiz settled in Mexico in 1568 and began working for Leonardo Fragoso, a printer of playing cards and of sacred pictures, so dear to humbler Roman Catholics of all countries and all times. Later, Ortiz went to work for Ocharte as a "cortador de imagenes" (*i.e.,* of sacred pictures). Ocharte's richly illustrated *Doctrina Christiana en Lengua Guasteca* contained not only older woodcuts, but also new ones never before used in any other Mexican book. The latter group includes four palms (of hands) with different arrangements of fingers on each, and may well have been the work of Ortiz. In 1572 the Holy Office apprehended Ortiz for allegedly heretical verses which appeared beneath a signed picture of Our Lady of the Rosary. The picture and the results of Ortiz's brain-washing are preserved in volume LI of the Inquisition Records in the Archivo Nacional in Mexico City. Whatever may have been the motives or the results of the activities of the Holy Office in the Americas, historians of the book would have been infinitely poorer in source materials if the investigating Fathers had not been so zealous and so meticulous in recording their findings.

After Espinosa and Ocharte came on the printing scene in Mexico, the quality and the quantity of book production increased perceptibly. Espinosa's great *Missale Romanum,* 1561, is one of the best designed books of the whole colonial period and is illustrated with portraits of religious personalities selected and portrayed with a well developed sense of propriety and of artistic merit. Ocharte used an unusually large number of woodcuts and elaborate initials. Pedro Balli, Mexico's fourth printer, borrowed type and woodcuts extensively from his predecessors and competitors and exchanged both with the latter. It is reasonable to assume that domestic wood engravers, some of them most certainly Indians or mestizos, began to work in Mexico before the end of the sixteenth century. For the next two centuries (1606–1802) Manuel Toussaint lists sixty-eight engravers.

In the seventeenth century copper engravings began to come into common use, probably the result of the immigration of foreign artists, such as Samuel Estradamus, a native of Antwerp, who was active in Mexico City from 1606 to 1622. Engravers began to sign their work, and we find many names frequently reappearing. Outstanding among them was Antonio de Castro, active from 1691 to 1732, who engraved both in copper and wood. His illustrations for Augustino de Mora's *El Sol Eclypsado antes de Llegar al Zenid,* and for the work of J. J. Guillena Carrascoso, were distinguished in a century which saw a true flowering of book illustration in Mexico. Francisco Silverio, who started his career in 1721 and continued for a quarter of a century, is another superior artist. His four plates measuring 48-1/2x56 em. for José Antonio Villaseñor y Sanchez, *Yconismo Hidroterro o Mapa Geographico de la America Septentrional,* 1750 are monumental and of high artistic quality.

The work of Mexican engravers of the latter half of the eighteenth century compares favorably with the best in Europe. José Mariano Navarro's impressive portrait of the Virgin of Guadalupe (perhaps the most popular subject for Mexican artists, even in our own century) is reproduced in the first volume of Medina's *His-*

toria de la Imprenta en los Antiguos Dominios Españoles de *America y Oceania*. The celebrated (and perhaps overrated) José Joaquín Fabregat, supervisor of engraving from 1788 until his death in 1807, in the Real Academia de las Tres Nobles Artes, San Carlos, did a handsome imitation of an engraving of Our Lady of Sorrows after Anton Raphael Mengs. It was produced for Diego Martínez's *Piadosos Recuerdos y Consideraciones de los Dolores de la Madre de Díos,* 1788. The Real Casa de Moneda was almost as fertile a training ground for young engravers as was the Real Academia in San Carlos.

A comprehensive, critical study of eighteenth century Mexican book illustration would be a desirable contribution which could be made to the history of the book in the Americas. We know the names of numerous artists and have some biographical data. Many, perhaps all, will finally be classified as epigoni, much as Fabregat, the imitator of Mengs. The European Rococo style dominated the Mexican book of the eighteenth century. Yet, there is also some originality, often even ingenuity, in the adaptation of traditional subjects to Mexican themes.

The earliest printers of Puebla de Los Angeles gave some attention to book illustration in the seventeenth century, but we have no evidence of local talent. We must assume that the cuts used in early Puebla came from the Peninsula or Mexico City. One of the earliest Puebla imprints, a *Sermon* of Bartolome Venavides y de la Cerda, printed in 1643, is dedicated to the great Bishop Juan de Palafox y Mendoza; the verso of the title page has a wood engraving of Palafox's armorial bearings. Palafox's own *Constituciones y Ordenanças del Colegio de San Juan Evangelista desta Ciudad de Los Angeles,* 1644, contains a wood engraving of St. John. Other books have similar illustrations of coats of arms, religious scenes and personalities, a noteworthy example being a portrait possibly of Sor Juana de la Cruz in Fray Juan Carrillo's *Vida y Prodigios de la Venerable Madre Sor Ivana de la Cruz,* 1684.

In 1695 we find a copper engraving of a coat of arms signed by one Miguel Amat in Antonio Delgado y Buenrostro's *Oracion Evangelica del Milagroso Indice de la Providencia,* but we do not know where he practiced his art. Neither do we have information about N. Villegas, who executed a copper engraving of Father

Juan Carnero for the biography by Joaquín Antonio de Villalobos, 1725, and additional work as late as 1766. José de Nava was probably the outstanding Puebla book illustrator, and we find numerous examples of his work from 1765 to 1807. Most distinguished are the thirty-three engravings he executed for a life of Santa Rosa de Viterbo, a book issued without a title-page. Other engravers who produced illustrations for Puebla printers and who may have resided there, signed the names Pérez, José Morales, N. Villavicencio, Troncoso, and Galicia. Their inspiration and theme was almost exclusively religious, and none showed exceptional originality.

The first book recorded by Medina in *La Imprenta en Guatemala 1660–1821,* 1910, is a *Sermon* of Fray Francisco de Quinones y Escobedo, printed by José de Pineda Ibarra in 1660. In the dedication we find the armorial bearings of Bishop Payo Enriquez de Ribera, who was responsible for bringing Pineda Ibarra to Guatemala and thus introduced the black art to the Captaincy General. We also find a wood engraving of the heraldic bearings of the Franciscans in the *Constituciones* of this order, 1662. Medina suspects that the engravings of these heraldic devices were the work of Pineda Ibarra or of the silversmiths resident in Guatemala. So far there is no other proof.

The first signed illustration in a Guatemalan book, that can be identified, is the frontispiece of Fray Francisco Vazquez's *Chronica de la Provincia del Santissimo Nõbre de Jesus de Guatemala* ... Guatemala, Imprenta de S. Francisco, 1714, engraved by Baltasar España. I have not seen this work and have only the statement of Medina that the engraving was in copper from "un buril no poco ejercitado". It is likely that this artist was an ancestor of José Casildo España, engraver of a sophisticated and imaginative portrait of the Eternal Father in the broadside of Manuel José Lara's *In Religionis Argumentum,* Guatemala, Beteta, 1801, of a portrait of Carol IV, 1801, and, *interalia,* of a "Plano General de la Ciudad de Guatemala". It is likely that another descendant is Apolinario España, whose *aqua fortis* map of Istapa, 1835, is the first of this genre in Guatemala. In 1739 one Blas de Avila signed an engraving of the crowned Virgin of Vicente Gutiérrez Talaban's *Maximum Denominationem Subit Opus,* Guatemala, Cristóbal de

Hincapié Meléndez, 1739. In 1746 we find his name under a masterful portrait (probably engraved in copper) of Saint Catherine in Raphael de Landibar Cavallero's *Secunda Fortuna*, Guatemala, Sebastian de Arevalo, 1746. In Fray Blas del Vallé's *Symbolica Oliva de Paz . . . Funeral . . . del Señor Don Fernando VI*, Guatemala, Arevalo, 1760, there is a conventional copper engraving of the tomb signed by José Valladares.

Pedro Garcia-Aguirre's career may be traced in large measure through the columns of the *Gazeta de Guatemala*. He worked in the Casa de Moneda in 1778 and in 1797 he was made Director of the "Escuela de Dibujo" which the Real Sociedad Económica opened in 1797 and he continued in that capacity for at least a decade. Many engravings of considerable skill, which were executed in this period, may be attributed to Garcia-Aguirre, *e.g.*, a portrait of Archbishop Francos y Monroy, 1780, the Virgin Mary, 1784, the Virgen del Socorro, 1785, and at least twenty other portraits, plans, maps, and designs. In the same period we find work signed by Casildo España, Juan José Rosales, Francisco Cabreras, and Narciso Rosal, artists whose work suggests that Guatemala was in close contact with current European techniques and styles of copper engraving. Cabrera worked under Garci-Aguirre in the Casa de Moneda and won distinction as an engraver of book illustrations and as a miniaturist. Garci-Aguirre's sons, Diego and Gonzalo, signed the twenty-seven engravings for the *Exequies of Carlos III* in 1789.

The quantity of Peruvian printing amounts to less than a third of that of Mexico during the colonial period. The typographical quality and the variety of illustrations in Peruvian books is, in general, inferior to the Mexican products. The *Doctrina Christiana y Catecísmo para Instrucción de los Indios*, 1584, is illustrated with cuts which Antonio Ricardo may well have brought with him from Mexico. Probably the first example of domestic illustration in Peru is the starkly simple portrait of Pedro de Oña in his *Arauco Domado*, Lima, 1596. Most likely this portrait, as well as a few other early illustrations in books printed by Ricardo were either his work or that of his assistants, Pareja and Almazán. Possibly some Lima silversmith may have made a contribution to the illustrations of Ricardo's books. We can only make assumptions at this stage of the investigation into the history of the book in colonial Spanish America.

Francisco del Canto Lozano, Lima's second printer, may have ordered from local artists the armorial bearings appearing in his books, but there are no signatures. Finally we find a signed engraving in 1613, when Lima's third printer, Pedro de Merchán y Calderón, produced Fray Martín de León's *Relación de las Exequias en la Muerte de la Reina Margarita* with a copper engraving of the imperial tomb, from a drawing by the author, and a frontispiece by Fray Francisco Bexerano. Bexerano may also have executed the engravings of the tomb erected in 1612 in the exequies of the Marqués de Montesclaros and of the title page of Fray Fernando de Valverde's *Santuario de Nuestra Señora de Copacabana en el Peru,* Lima, 1641. For the next half century only sporadic wood engravings appear in Peruvian books. No professional engraver or illustrator seems to have settled in Lima. In 1666 the signature of P. A. Delhom appeared on a copper engraving in the *Aclamación y Pendones que Levanto la . . . Ciudad de los Reyes por el Católico Carlos II.* and on the frontispiece of the *Solemnidad Fúnebre de Felipe IV,* but no other works are known to have come from his burin. In 1676 a Mercedarian friar, Pedro Nolasco de Mere, engraved two copper plates with views of the Sanctuary of Saint Francis and in 1685 a neatly detailed plan of Lima. Some years later this artist produced the remarkable "Cristo del Milagro" which Medina calls "one of the most noteworthy engravings executed in Lima during the Spanish domination". It measures 16x26 cm. and shows Christ and the Virgin standing, Magdalene kneeling and the City of Jerusalem in the distance. Several other engravings signed by Nolasco have survived.

It is unfortunate that the engraver of the plates for the richly illustrated *Historia de España* by Peralta Barnuevo, 1730, did not sign his work. Medina speculates that it may have been Father Nolasco de Mere, or possibly the Dominican Friar Miguel Adame, whose first known work is a portrait of Saint Rita in 1699; he signed several other pieces. Other illustrators who can be identified were Michael Hierónimo, Antonio de Contreras, Cristóbal Garrido, José Vázquez, Marcelo Cavello, and Domingo Ayala. Most of their work was routine and imitative, although special mention should be made of Cavello, who made an honest effort to engrave a realistic portrait of the Viceroy O'Higgins, which accompanies a sonnet to him.

Lima's contribution to colonial Spanish American typography and illustration was relatively undistinguished. The productions of Mexico and even Guatemala and remote Paraguay were more significant. It would be hazardous to speculate on reasons, although unsettled political conditions certainly played a role in this situation. A careful study of the early manifestations of the graphic arts in Peru should be an exciting adventure for an inquisitive bibliographer of colonial Hispanic America.

In the entire history of the graphic arts there is no story more remarkable than that of the origins of engraving and painting in the Jesuit "reductions" (reducciones are settlements of "pacified and civilized" Indians) of old Paraguay (a geographical term applied in the seventeenth and eighteenth centuries not only to the country between the Paraguay and Paraná Rivers, but also to nearby territories of Brazil, Argentina, and Uruguay). The Jesuits taught many European arts and crafts to their Guaraní wards in the theocratic-communistic state they established, and began to think about importing a printing press as early as 1633. However, a normal lifetime was to elapse before printing actually came to old Paraguay.

In the meanwhile the Jesuit fathers were not to be without books, and therefore they had books. They taught the Guaranís to copy European printed books by meticulously imitating type and illustrations. Father Francisco Xarque or Jarque observed in his *Insignes Missioneros de la Compañia de Jesus en la Provincia del Paraguay,* Pamplona, 1687, that the Indians could copy a Missal printed in Antwerp with such accuracy that it was difficult to distinguish their manuscripts from the printed books. Father Guillermo Fúrlong Cárdiff, in his monumental *Historia y Bibliografía de las primeras Imprentas Rioplatensis, 1700–1850,* 1953, refers to a manuscript book of this sort in the Museo Mitre at Buenos Aires, dated 1696, four years before the first book was printed in Paraguay. Most remarkable, however, is a manuscript copy of the *Decadas* of Nicolás del Techo in the Biblioteca Nacional of Madrid (no. 5931, formerly Q-316). Thirty or more Indians did this job, and both the type and the engravings were copied with deceptive accuracy, judging from the illustration in Father Fúrlong's study.

Even more interesting is the work of the Guaraní xylographers. There is reason to believe that the Jesuits of old Paraguay had their Indians make engravings for xylographic broadsides, pamphlets, and even whole books. An impression from a woodblock found in Paraguay and presently in the Biblioteca Enrique Peña in Argentina is reproduced by Fúrlong. This type of engraving and printing may well have been done by the Guaranís in the seventeenth century, although this particular block should probably be dated subsequent to the expulsion of the Jesuits in 1767.

The first surviving printed book from Paraguay shows a wealth of illustrations. Father Juan Eusebio Nieremberg's *De la Diferencia entre lo Temporal y Eterno,* Impreso en las Doctrinas, 1705, is a volume of 438 pages in double columns, completely in Guaraní. The book contains forty-three plates and seventy-seven vignettes and initials illustrating scenes from the life of Christ. Designed and engraved in a style worthy of the leading book artists of seventeenth century Europe, the illustrations hardly seem to be of the quality that one expects to have been produced in the steaming jungles of Paraguay. Many of the plates, to be sure, are copied from European works, but when juxtaposing the engravings copied from Europe and the original Paraguayan work reproduced in Furlong, Nieremberg's book becomes even more fantastic. One of the most striking illustrations is a portrait of the Jesuit General Tirso González; it is signed: "Joan Yapari sculps—Doctrinas Paraquariae". The history of American art is infinitely poorer for the lack of information on the life and other work of Juan Yapari.

Of the other eight surviving titles from the early Paraguayan press, none are illustrated as extensively as the first. The Indian Nicolás Yapuguai's *Explicación de el Catechismo,* Santa Maria La Mayor, 1724, has a moving and singularly American looking Virgin and Child on the title page, undoubtedly local work.

Six publications of the short-lived Jesuit press in Córdoba de Tucumán have survived. All are dated 1766 and 1767 and contain several carefully executed borders, initials, and armorial devices. In the pamphlet containing the *Reglas* of the Colegio de Montserrat, the main Jesuit establishment in Córdoba, there is a rather handsome engraving of the Virgin of Montserrat. It is likely that all of these ornaments and illustrations were engraved on wood in Córdoba. Such an assumption is reasonable until evidence of their prior use in some other part of the world can be found.

Printing did not come to Buenos Aires until 1780. The great majority of the early Buenos Aires imprints were broadsides, Novenas, and short official documents. There was a tasteful use of type ornaments (most of them imported, some possibly domestic). Rodolfo Trostiné states in his *El Grabado en la Argentina durante el Período Hispánico*, 1949, that the earliest Argentine engraving known is a little vessel on a shipping dispatch, "Conocimientos para el Despacho de las Naos, que van a los Reynos Castilla", 1760, probably stamped on paper by hand. The first Argentine book illustration is in Fray Eugenio de la Santísima Trinidad, *Trisagio Seráfica, para Venerar a la muy Augusta y Santa Trinidad*, 1781, a copper engraving of the Holy Trinity by a silversmith named Juan Antonio Callejas y Sandoval. Another early Buenos Aires engraver who produced illustrations for almanacs was Pedro Carmona. A rather handsome and original engraving dated 1783 shows Saint Benedict of Palermo, and could be the work of Callejas y Sandoval or possibly of Manuel Rivera, who drew an imaginative Virgin of Lluján, popular well into the next century.The original copper plate for the Saint Benedict is in the Biblioteca Enrique Peña. Probably the only wood engraving of any consequence that was produced in Buenos Aires in the eighteenth century (so Medina says) is a little Virgin of the Rosary in the *Novena. A la Rosa Mystica*, 1796.

Book illustration in eighteenth century Argentina is infrequent, and most illustrations lack depth and sense of movement. Just before the wars of independence a handsome portrait of Ferdinand VII was engraved by Juan de Dios Rivera, an employee of the Casa de Moneda in Potosí. Finally, mention should be made of the "Santa Rita de Casia", 1809, a lively copy full of originality of the European examples by Manuel Pablo Nuñez de Ibarra. Most of Nuñez de Ibarra's work was done after 1810.

The history of printing in that part of the Kingdom of New Granada which is now Colombia requires much more intensive investigation than it has received so far. Medina's bibliography of early Bogotá printing is fragmentary, and Eduardo Posada's *Bibliografía Bogotana,* 1917, leaves much to be desired from the standpoint of meticulous description. When the definitive bibliography of early Colombian printing is compiled, we will be in a much more favorable position to study book illustration; meanwhile Gabriel Giraldo Jaramillo's *El Grabado en Colombia,* published in 1960, will be useful.

Some tastefully used type ornaments and vignettes were used in the ten known Jesuit imprints of Bogotá from 1738 to 1742; otherwise the designs of the Septenarios and Novenas were as austere as their texts. The next printing in Bogotá, beginning in 1777 by Antonio Espinosa de los Monteros, was aptly characterized by Medina as "pobre probrísimo". This epithet was correct by instinct only, since Medina, who published his Bogotá bibliography in 1904, uncovered only a fraction of the imprints that Posada listed thirteen years later. Neither bibliography records illustrations of any importance.

In 1782 Francisco Benito de Miranda, an employee of the Casa de Moneda in Bogotá, executed a charming copper engraving of "La Divina Pastora", an enduring monument of the Marian cult in Colombia (illustrated in Giraldo Jaramillo). In the same year was published an edict of the noted Archbishop Viceroy Antonio Caballero y Góngora with his armorial bearings engraved in copper at the end. Giraldo Jaramillo attributes them to Benito de Miranda "sin duda alguna". Other surviving work of Benito de Miranda includes two versions of the celebrated Virgin of the Rosary of Chiquinquirá.

In 1785 appeared a Rosary with a cross and two keys on the title page. In 1787 a coat of arms on the title page of the *Capitulos de las Reales Ordenanzas de la Renta de Corresos;* and Medina speaks of a "grabadito" in Asula y Lozano's *Historia del Christo Paciente* of the same year, a book I have not seen. In 1802 appeared in Bogotá a pamphlet entitled *Origin y Descubrimiento de la Vaccina* with an engraving showing a nurse vaccinating a patient, the first Colombian print with a secular theme. There are two other illustrations in this work. In 1804 we find a rather primitive wood engraving of the Virgin of the Snows and in 1806 one of the Virgin of Sorrows, both reproduced by Giraldo Jaramillo. The first native Colombian engraver was Anselmo García de Tejada, an employee of the Casa de Moneda. The only work from his hand that survives is a copper engraving of Nuestro Señora de la Peña, 1818, of which Giraldo Jaramillo reproduces an unique copy from his own collection. Almost half a century before printing was introduced to the westernmost part of the old Kingdom of New Granada, now Ecuador, a remarkable map of the Amazon basin was drawn in Quito in 1707 by Father Samuel Fritz, a Jesuit priest born in Bohemia. Fritz's map was engraved and printed in Quito by Father Juan de Narváez in the same year. There is a facsimile in A.A.M. Stols, *Historia de la Imprenta en el Ecuador de 1755–1830,* 1953. Narváez was also responsible for a religious engraving, designed with the collaboration of Fray Miguel de Santa Cruz and the well known painter, Nicolás Javier de Goríbar, which was drawn to illustrate some theological conclusions in the Colegio Máximo in Quito. I have not seen this engraving and am depending on Father Fúrlong's essay: *Un Grabado Quiteño de 1718,* which he presented at the Second International Congress of History of the Americas, published in the third volume of the *Proceedings.* Narváez also engraved a gallery of Inca rulers in 1714 based on the sketches of Lic. Alonso de la Cueva, chronicler of the Cathedral of Lima. Other early eighteenth-century engravings in Ecuador have been described by Father José María Vargas in his article *Algunos Datos Históricos sobre el Grabado en el Ecuador* in *El Comercio* (Quito), 22 March 1953.

The Jesuits apparently maintained a regular engraving atelier in colonial Quito. Father Jacinto Morán de Butrón ordered there a collection of plates of which twenty comprised an historical Catechism, twenty-three the Mass, and twenty-five the Life of Christ. In addition to Father Narváez, two other engravers, Simón Brieva and Miguel de Santa Cruz, are mentioned by Father Vargas. Brother Miguel, born in Cuenca in 1663 and active as late as 1742, is the first native Ecuadorean engraver. One other Ecuadorean engraver prior to the book-printing period is Brother José Iglesias, who executed a portrait of Loyola in Quito in 1743.

The first book illustration proper that can be identified in an Ecuadorean imprint is described in Stols' number four, the *Devoción a los SS. Corazones de Jesus y María,* printed in Ambato in 1756 by Juan Adán Schwartz. In 1762, after the press moved to

Quito, we find a copper engraving of Saint Nicholas in the *Novena al Glorioso San Nicolás*. Beginning with 1780 there are some copper engravings signed by "R.S." and Joaquín Cruz. The temptation is strong to ascribe the initials to Raimundo de Salazar, who succeeded Schwartz after the Jesuit expulsion of 1767 and operated the press with skill and competence until 1793. Stols identifies twenty-two book illustrations or illustrated printed broadsides in the seventy-seven years covered in his bibliography. It is, to be sure, a slender production, but the quality is relatively high, thanks to the early tradition and quality of engraving in Ecuador and also because of the competence of Schwartz and Salazar as designers and pressmen.

The first book illustration in Cuba came at an early date in the history of printing on that island. Carlos Habré, who printed the first three books in Cuba in 1723, 1724, and 1727, illustrated the last of this group, Francisco Mendez Marquez's *Rubricas Generales del Breviario Romano,* with a crude wood engraving which, Medina suspects, he himself may have cut. Not until 1762 do we discover another illustration in a Cuban book, a copper engraving signed by one Bélez, of whom we know nothing. It is the *Relación y Diario de la Previsión* of Bishop Morel de Santa Cruz, 1762, and shows the violent removal of that unfortunate prelate from his episcopal palace.

Few Havana imprints were illustrated. Antonio Parra's *Descripción de Diferentes Píezas de Historia Natural,* 1787, is a noteworthy exception. It contains seventy-seven plates, in some copies colored, executed with considerable skill and scientific knowledge by the son of the author. In general, however, the rather slight printing and publishing business of eighteenth and early nineteenth century Havana was far from sufficient in volume to support a full-time engraver. (Medina records only 266 imprints in Havana through 1810, some of which are surely ghosts.) Any competent engraver had to go to Mexico City to make a living. By the same reason engravings for religious pieces printed in Havana were probably imported from Mexico.

At the other extreme of Hispanic colonization of the Americas we find that the aristocratic German Jesuit Carlos Haimhausen brought a printing press to Chile in 1747. Unfortunately, nothing is known to have been printed on it before the expulsion of the Jesuits in 1767. In 1776 an extremely crude nine-page pamphlet entitled *Modo de Canar el Jubileo Santo* was printed in Santiago, but regular printing did not begin in Chile until 1780. Medina counted twenty-one pieces, mainly official broadsides, between 1780 and 1811, but these were undistinguished typographically. By 1811 we find a Royal Coat of Arms and a crude wood engraving used by a Chilean printer, but book illustration proper did not exist in Chile in the colonial period. The first volume of the famous *Aurora de Chile*, issued in 1812 under the editorship of Fray Camilo Henriquez, has a crude woodcut on the title page. The graphic arts were slow to take roots in Chile, and illustration became common only after independence.

In retrospect the illustration of colonial Spanish American books was based on a relatively weak tradition. The total volume of Spanish American printing before 1810 is comparable to the total volume of fifteenth century European printing, but there is a vast difference in the quality and quantity of illustration. Only one center, Mexico City, had a strong indigenous group of artists. A few could be found in the latter part of the eighteenth century in Guatemala, Puebla, and Lima. Until the end of the colonial period many of the best artists were clergymen who had been educated in Europe. Styles were largely imitative.

There are exceptions to this rather discouraging picture. The fantastic story of printing and copying in the Reducciones of old Paraguay might have been the start of a great artistic tradition if printing had not stopped abruptly after a couple of decades. A few individuals such as Silverio, Navarro, and Pedro Nolasco de Mere revealed sparks of genius, but they founded no school or tradition. Still, we do not yet know enough about colonial Spanish American book illustration to draw any final conclusions.

The corpus of book illustration is small enough to warrant a comprehensive work on the order of Schramm's *Bilderschmuck der Frühdrucke,* 1920–1943. Such work, together with further investigations as to the indentities and careers of the illustrators and engravers, would surely constitute a major contribution to the general history of bookish culture and art in the old Spanish colonies of America.

Some Reconsiderations of the Origin of Printing in Sixteenth-Century Mexico*

Perhaps the most important surviving document on the origins of printing in Mexico is the contract of 12 June 1539 between Juan Cromberger ("impresor") and Juan Pablos ("cajista") in which the conditions of Pablos' operation are specified.[1] There are several transcriptions, of which the most readily accessible is possibly the one in García Icazbalceta's *Bibliografía mexicana del siglo XVI.* [2] The specifications set forth by the prosperous Cromberger firm are rather exacting but intelligible with a single exception. Cromberger stated that Pablos should organize his presswork so that he would be "haziendo la tarea de tres mill pliegos cada dia, como se faze en la dicha vuestra casa. . ." (printing three thousand sheets each day, as is done in your shop).

Literally interpreted, "tres mill pliegos cada dia" simply could not be printed in a day of twenty-four hours on one press. There are numerous records of the known output of pressmen on the presses in use in the sixteenth and seventeenth centuries. One source only will be cited, D.F. McKenzie's *The Cambridge University Press 1696–1712,*[3] in which there are meticulous records of the operation of the Cambridge press. The daily average of sheets produced by one pressman ranged from 167 to 1,017; by two pressmen, from 655 to 1,725.

The specification of three thousand sheets a day has frequently caused some astonishment among students of Mexican prototypo-

*Reprinted with permission of the publisher from *Homage to a Bookman,* Essays on Manuscripts, Books, and Maps for Hans P. Kraus on His Sixtieth Birthday, October 12, 1967 (Berlin, Gebrüder Mann, 1967), pp. 183-186.

graphy, but no one has yet offered a satisfactory explanation. In any event, Pablos' actual production—even assuming maximum editions and unknown works—was far less than 3,000 sheets a day. So we are still without an explanation for the careful legal language in the contract.

No reasonable explanation of the curious phrase should be eliminated; but one, that of a scribal error ("mill" for "cientos" or "día" for "semana") seems to be less likely in view of the meticulous composition of the document as a whole. Further, there is no lexicographical evidence of any variant meanings for "mill," "día," or "pliegos" in sixteenth-century Spanish. Another unlikely possibility is that Pablos and Cromberger could have been thinking of 3,000 *impressions* on 1,500 sheets, recto and verso; it is doubtful that two experienced printers would have spoken in these terms.

The contract was a hard one for Pablos, and it is not impossible that Cromberger set an unreasonable standard of production simply to keep his equipment in maximum production during the decade when it was in the custody of Pablos. Pablos was accompanied by his wife, Gerónima Gutierres (or Nuñez), apparently a fairly young and vigorous woman, who, according to the contract, was "obligada o rregir e servir la casa en todo lo que fuere menester" (responsible for managing and serving the shop in every necessary detail). Also he took with him his "oficial Gil Barbero y . . . un esclavo negro, Llamado Pedro"[4] (employee Gil Barbero and . . . a negro slave called Pedro). Cromberger might have argued that if one able pressman in his shop could produce 750 sheets, four could produce 3,000 ("como se faze en la dicha vuestra casa").

As we have seen from the Cambridge figures, it is not out of the question for a team of two pressmen to print 1,500 sheets a day; but they would surely keep at least one press in full operation. Could there have been another printing press in Mexico when Pablos began his operations?

When Juan de Zumárraga, bishop of Mexico since 1528, was in the metropolis in 1533 and 1534, he undoubtedly conferred with the new viceroy, Antonio de Mendoza (who did not establish his residence in New Spain until 1535), about the spiritual and intellectual needs of his episcopate. A printing press was surely in the minds of both men; and there is a memorandum from Zumárraga in the Archivo de Indias about the need for a press and a paper mill in Mexico.[5] There is no direct evidence that Zumárraga negotiated with Cromberger; but the latter, as the main printer in the port of exit for the Indies, would have been a logical agent.

We do not know when and how a press was sent to Mexico, we only know that at least one was sent by Cromberger;[6] and that there is no positive evidence of a press in New Spain before 6 May 1538. On this date Zumárraga wrote to the Emperor:

> Poco se puede adelantar en lo de la imprenta por la carestía del papel, que éste dificulta las muchas obras que acá están aparejadas y otras que habrán de nuevo darse a la estampa, pues que se carece de las más necesarias, y de allá son pocos las que vienen.[7]
>
> (Little progress can be made with the business of printing because of the lack of paper, since this situation puts obstacles in the way of many works which are being prepared here and others, which ought to be reprinted, since the most essential things are lacking and little equipment comes from abroad.)

There is no other documentation to indicate the presence of a press or a printer in New Spain before this date. However, arguments have been advanced forcefully (and rebutted with equal vigor) to prove there was a printing press and a printer in Mexico before 1538 and that he practiced his craft.[8]

There is substantial evidence that there was a printer in New Spain possibly as early as 1536 or even before. At some time between 28 April 1536 and 1538 the precentor of the cathedral of Mexico, Cristóbal de Pedrazo, was in Spain and at that time he wrote a memorandum to the king advising "que un maestro imprimidor tiene voluntad de servir a V. M. con su arte, y pasar a la Nueva España a empremir allá libros de yglesia. . ." (that a master printer is willing to serve Your Majesty with his craft, and to go to New Spain and print books of the church there).[9] Medina thought that one Esteban Martín was this master printer, that he may have arrived in Mexico as early as 1534, and that he was at work from 1535 to 1538. It is of some interest to note that on 5 September 1539— some sixteen months after Zumárraga complained of the slow progress of printing in Mexico—there is a record of the acceptance of one Esteban Martín, *impresor,* as a *vecino* (denizen) of the city of Mexico.[10] It should be noted that final confirmation of the status of *vecindad* (denizenation) usually did not take place until after some years of residence.

If Martín actually printed, not a scrap of anything from his press is known today. Medina and those who accept his idea about Martín's activities as a printer think that he printed an alleged Spanish edition of Joannes Climachus, *Scala Páradisi,* Torrebelvicino, 19 Sept. 1477 (H 5466), the *Escala spiritual* by San Juan Climaco. Dávila Padilla refers to such a book, although he attributes it to Juan Pablos.[11] Alonso Fernandez also attributes it to Pablos but assigns to it the specific date of 1535,[12] and González Dávila dates it 1532, the year to which he also assigns, incorrectly, the arrival of Viceroy Mendoza.[13] Medina believed that only Martín could have been the printer of the *Escala spiritual* and offers strong arguments to support this contention. Conclusive evidence is lacking.

If the press sent by Cromberger was in addition to one sent earlier, four pressmen might have been expected to print 3,000 sheets daily under optimum circumstances (likely to have been assumed by an imperious employer such as Cromberger). Millares Carlo and Julián Calvo point out in their monograph on *Juan Pablos, primer impresor que a esta tierra vino,*[14] that the contract between Pablos and Cromberger makes no mention of Zumárraga or Mendoza and their interest in the spiritual welfare of New Spain. Actually, there was no special need for such a reference in a purely business document.

There is a strong possibility that there were two presses in Mexico when Juan Pablos began to print and that Cromberger was aware of this situation when he dictated the contract of 12 June 1539. To have specified 3,000 sheets a day from a single press would have been patently ridiculous to veteran printers. If there was a press sent to Mexico before May 1538, we have no evidence that it was used for at least a year. Indeed, there is a suggestion to the contrary in Zumárraga's complaint about the slow process of getting a printing press into operation. If Pablos knew of its existence, he might not have been too reluctant to agree to produce 3,000 sheets a day when he was thinking of a rosy business future in the New World with three pressmen besides himself at his disposal.

NOTES

1. Seville, Archivo notarial, Protocolo de Alonso de la Barrera, Oficio I, Libro I de 1539, fol. 1069. A photographic copy of the original is in the University of Kentucky Library, secured for the writer through the good offices of Professor Magnus Mörner and the courtesy of the Archivo de Indias.

2. New ed. by Agustín Millares Carlo, Mexico, Fondo de cultura económica, 1954, pp. 42-5, with references. A comparison with the photograph indicates that this transcription is accurate.

3. Cambridge, At the University Press, 1966; 2 vols.; Table 14, vol. I, pp. 132-3.

4. Seville, Archivo notarial, Protocolo de Alonso de la Barrera, Oficio I, Libro I de 1539, fol. 1069, also dated 12 June 1539.

5. Seville, Archivo de Indias, Sección V, Audiencia de México, legajo 2555; *cf.* also José Toribio Medina, *La imprenta en México* (1539-1821), Santiago de Chile, Impreso en casa del autor, 1908-12, 8 vols., vol. I, p. xxxvi, and García Icazbalceta, *Don fray Juan de Zumárraga, primer obispo y arzobispo de México; estudio biográfico y bibliográfico,* Mexico, Andrade y Morales, 1881, pp. 466-7.

6. See the *cédula real* dated Talavera, 6 June 1542, reprinted by García Icazbalceta, *Bibliografía mexicana del siglo XVI,* pp. 45-6, from the original in the Archivo General de México, Libro II de Mercedes, ff. 48r-49v, actually ff. 46r-47 v, expediente 120.

7. *Cartas de Indias* (Madrid, 1877) p. 786, col. 2; also in García Icazbalceta, *Don fray Juan de Zumárraga,* apendice, no. 25.

8. At this point it is unnecessary to review fully the controversy started by Francisco Vindel, *El primer libro impreso en America fué para El rezo del Santo Rosario,* Madrid, 1953, and the subsequent rebuttals and answers. Suffice it to say, some scholars accept the possibility that this prayer of the rosary may have been printed in Mexico.

9. Seville, Archivo de Indias; cited by García Icazbalceta, *Bibliografía mexicana del siglo XVI,* p. 42, and Medina, *op. cit.,* vol. I, p. xlviii.

10. Mexico, Archivo de la Ciudad, Libro IV de las Actas del Cabildo, 1536-1539, f. 124r; facsimile and transcription in Emilio Valtón, *Impresos mexicanos del siglo xvi (incunables mexicanos) en la Biblioteca Nacional le México, el Museo Nacional y el Archivo General de la Nación; con cincuenta y dos láminas; estudio bibliográfico precedido de una introducción sobre los orígenes de la imprenta en América* (Mexico, Imprenta universitaria, 1935), pl. 1 and p. 7.

11. Agustín Dávila Padilla, *Historia de la fundación y discurso de la Provincia de Santiago de México*, Madrid, 1596, p. 670.

12. Alonso Fernández, *Historia eclesiástica de nuestros tiempos*, Toledo, por la viuda de P. Rodriguez, 1611, p. 122.

13. Gil Gonzáles Dávila, *Teatro eclesiástico de la primitiva iglesia de las Indias Occidentales*, Madrid, D. Diaz de la Carrera, 1649-55; 2 vols, vol. I, p. 23.

14. Agustin Millares Carlo and Julián Calvo, *Juan Pablos primer impresor que a esta tierra vino*, Mexico, Libreria, de Manuel Porrúa, 1953.

PART TWO

LIBRARIES OF THE
CARIBBEAN

The Libraries of Puerto Rico[*]

Lawrence S. Thompson and Jorge Rivera Ruiz

The beginnings of libraries in Puerto Rico go back far into Spanish colonial times, but circumstances have not favored a continuing tradition of books and readers on this hurricane-swept island neglected for four centuries by the Spaniards. Numerous private and public collections of considerable importance have been lost or damaged in storms and earthquakes, and the almost perpetual economic distress has been rather unfavorable to cultural development of any sort.

As early as 1523 the first library was organized in the Convento de Santo Domingo (at the entrance to Fort Brooke, or "El Morro," San Juan), but it was destroyed by the Dutch in 1625.[1] It has further been intimated that a music library of some proportions existed in the Cathedral of San Juan prior to 1598, when Lord George Clifford, Earl of Cumberland, carried away the organ and bells of the cathedral after looting the city. It is definitely known that a music library was reassembled in 1660 when the church created the position of organist and choir leader for the Cathedral of San Juan.[2]

The Dutch invasion of 1625 destroyed not only the library of the Convento de Santo Domingo but also other book collections and the archives of the episcopate. Especially regrettable was the destruction of the library of Bishop Bernardo de Valbuena

*Reprinted with permission of the University of Chicago Press from *The Library Quarterly*, XVI (1946), 225-238.

(1568—1627), bishop of Puerto Rico from 1620 until his death.[3] Lope celebrated this famous collection in verse:

> Y siempre dulce tu memoria sea,
> Generoso prelado,
> Doctísimo Bernardo de Valbuena.
> Tenías tú el cayado
> De Puerto Rico cuando el fiero Enrique,
> Holandés rebelado,
> Robó tu librería;
> Pero tu ingenio no, que no podía,
> Aunque las fuerzas del olvido aplique.
> Qué bien cantaste al español Bernardo!
> Qué bien al *Siglo de Oro!*
> Tú fuiste su prelado y su tesoro,
> Y tesoro tan rico en Puerto Rico,
> Que nunca Puerto Rico fué tan rico.[4]

After the disastrous attack by the Dutch the Franciscans organized a library in about 1650,[5] but the books disappeared when the community was dissolved in 1835.[6] There are no definite records of organized libraries in eighteenth-century Puerto Rico; but since it is known that the Dominicans[7] as well as the Franciscans were teaching courses in theology, law, and Latin, it is most probable that this instruction was supported by libraries of some sort.

Far more significant than the work of the religious orders was the foundation of the (Real) Sociedad Económica de Amigos del País in 1813,[8] As early as 1843 the Sociedad Económica was moving toward the foundation of a library. In this year the cleric Dr. Don Rufo Manuel Fernández gave a "small but select" collection to the Sociedad, and a special cabinet was built to house these books.[9] Apparently no real progress was made by the Sociedad in organizing its library until 1863, when Federico Asenjo's bimonthly *El Fomento de Puerto Rico*[10] announced the founding of a public library and a scientific museum. This institution of truly democratic inspiration proposed to serve as a center for the dissemination of news, a continuation school, and a folk high school of humanistic studies. We have no figures on the extent of its collections or the degree to which it was used; and we only know that when the Sociedad was dissolved in 1899, its collections were divided between the Ateneo Puertorriqueño (founded 1876) and the newly founded insular library.[11]

During the nineteenth century a good deal more vitality was revealed by the other popular libraries, the so-called "bibliotecas municipales," founded in Mayagüez, San Juan, and Ponce during the latter part of the nineteenth century. The first of the group was the Biblioteca Municipal of Mayagüez, founded in 1873.[12] On October 13, 1873, the Consejo Municipal of that city ordered the investment of a thousand Spanish pesetas in the library, and on January 12, 1874, this sum was augmented by 3,250 pesetas. On March 15, 1874, this first true public library in Puerto Rico was opened. Del Toro states that the first librarian was Don Francisco del Castillo; but Don Adolfo Ruiz, an old resident of Mayagüez, says that one Alfredo Vigo was the custodian of the collection at this time. No one in the library or the city administration at present can supply any information to clarify this point. At all events, the library prospered and grew from 879 volumes in 1874 to 3,860 in 1913. On October 12, 1918, the devastating earthquake which rocked Mayagüez virtually destroyed the collection. The present collection of the Biblioteca Municipal can be said to be a new library for all practical purposes.

Don Manuel Fernández Juncos, for many years librarian of the Carnegie Library in San Juan and an outstanding man of letters, used to tell a rather picturesque tale of the beginnings of the Biblioteca Municipal of San Juan. According to him, this collection dates from 1879, when a group of friends meeting in the residence of Don Manuel Elzaburu, founder of the Ateneo Puertorriqueño, expressed a good deal of concern over the lack of a popular library to supplement the educational activities of the Ateneo. Don Manuel contributed twenty-five books, and others contributed in like manner to promote the founding of the new library. Don Venancio Luiña, a wealthy merchant, contributed an ounce of gold with which books selected by the editor of *El Buscapie* were purchased. On October 16, 1880, San Juan's Biblioteca Municipal was opened in the basement of the Casa Municipal with some five hundred volumes.

A significant commentary on the backwardness of libraries during the Spanish regime in Puerto Rico may be found in the early history of the San Juan Biblioteca Municipal. Among the books bought with Don Venancio's money was a complete set of Jovellanos. When a list of the library's holdings was published in the local press, a clerical periodical attempted to have the set of Jovellanos purged from the library. Fortunately the attempt was unsuccessful.[13] Again, in 1884, the Ayuntamiento of San Juan, alarmed by the contents of some of the books given to the municipal library, initiated a sort of censorship which, according to contemporary opinion, lacked the proper attributes for carrying out its delicate task.[14]

At all events, the new library prospered under the direction of Don Ramón Santaella, a gifted raconteur and as energetic in his pursuit of gift material as he was scornful of conventional library methods. Beginning with some four hundred volumes in 1880, the new library had more than six thousand by 1910, according to Pedreira.[15] Unlike the municipal libraries of Ponce and Mayagüez, the Biblioteca Muncipal of San Juan was a circulating library when it was first founded, but today the situation is reversed. San Juan lends no books, whereas Ponce and Mayagüez do.

In one sense the Biblioteca Municipal of Ponce is the oldest of the three, even though it opened its doors only in 1890. It was based on a *gabinete de lectura* founded in 1870 by Alejandro Tapia y Rivera and other contemporary literary figures.[16] In 1890 this *gabinete* was combined with gifts from Don Miguel Rosich's private collection to form the Biblioteca Municipal under the librarianship of Don Joaquin Figueroa. Pedreira had access to figures showing that the Biblioteca Municipal of Ponce started with 809 books and 669 pamphlets; and according to Del Toro this library had 2,818 volumes and 1,936 pamphlets by 1913.

Other municipal librbraries have been founded from time to time in various towns of Puerto Rico. Most of them were just on the borderline of being *gabinetes de lectura*. In the early 1900's Yauco constructed the first building in Puerto Rico which was devoted exclusively to library purposes,[17] but a recent visit to that town revealed that the building has been demolished, and not even a picture of it is available today. When Arthur E. Gropp surveyed the libraries of Puerto Rico in 1940, he reported rumors of a municipal library in San Germán, but this allegation could not be substantiated after exhaustive inquiries in that ancient city.[18]. Cayey, Fajardo, Guayama, and other towns are said to have had municipal libraries at one time or another, but if they did, they have suffered the same fate as the one at Yauco. A few collections along the lines of the old-fashioned Sunday-school library in the United States, and never containing more than a couple of hundred tracts and religiously inspired novels, have been established by the energetic Redemptorist Fathers, a North American order active in Puerto Rico.

Puerto Rico is not the most fertile ground for the municipal public library of the North American type. Above all else there is the overwhelming problem of illiteracy. Ismael Rodriguez Bou, secretary of the Consejo Superior de Enseñanza in Rio Piedras, cites figures to 31.5 per cent, putting Puerto Rico behind only Chile, Uruguay, and Argentina among the Latin American jurisdictions.[19] But formal statistics are misleading. For example, it was found in an informal private survey that out of a group of 162 selective service registrants only 51 were listed as illiterate. Actually, it was found that 63 others had signed their registration cards after a fashion, claimed two or three years of school, otherwise were unable to write and able to read only the most elementary signs. Nevertheless, the latter group was carried as literate by the various boards.

A truer tale of Puerto Rican literacy and reading habits was revealed by Charles C. Rogler in his study of Puerto Rico's Middletown, Comerío.[20] When Rogler made his study he found that only seventy-eight copies of *El Mundo*, leading Puerto Rican daily newspaper, were sold in Comerío daily, although the population of this typical hill town was 16,715 in 1930. There are no local publications. Except for two priests and a few school teachers in the town, nobody reads much. Private libraries are restricted to a few dusty collections of fourth-rate subscription books in the back rooms of upper middle-class homes.

The late Antonio S. Pedreira, perhaps the most penetrating analyst of Puerto Rican culture who has ever studied the island's history critically, stated frankly:

Rarísimos son los municipios que en sus presupuestos demuestran amor al libro. Es, además, muy cuesta arriba hacerles comprender que una biblioteca municipal es tan importante como una plaza de mercado o un matadero.[21]

When Gropp investigated the municipal libraries of Puerto Rico just prior to the war, he found a total of 2,527 volumes in Ponce's Biblioteca Municipal, and it was estimated that there were some nine thousand in San Juan's Biblioteca Municipal. Neither at that time nor subsequently has it been possible to determine the numerical statistics of Mayagüez' holdings. Thus, with the exception of the Carnegie Library in San Juan, he could report less than twenty thousand books available to the two million people of Puerto Rico; and these small collections were concentrated in "metropolitan" centers containing barely 20 per cent of the population.

Apparently the Biblioteca Municipal of San Juan has shrunk considerably since Gropp made his survey. As of the summer of 1945 it was reported to contain 5,661 volumes, mostly of historical, religious, and literary content. Very few have a recent imprint date, and there is little up-to-date reference material. The books are not classified, and the catalog locates the books by means of a shelf mark. In 1945–46, $16,680 was appropriated for the library, but only $3,000 was for the purchase of books. Appointments to the library staff are generally alleged to be made on the basis of political affiliations, and there are no employees with any technical library training. There are two branches, one in Puerta de Tierra (about a mile away) and one in Santurce (about two miles away).

Today the Biblioteca Municipal of Ponce is officially known as the Biblioteca Pública. It is maintained under the joint auspices of the Lions Club and the Ponce section of the Asociación Bibliotecaria de Puerto Rico (a kind of a "friends of the library" organization rather than a true professional association). Its revenues are derived from the Lions, the insular government (which contributed $4,484 in 1945), and fees levied on readers ($1,301 secured from this source in 1942). The collection is said to amount to 9,648 volumes of a general character, and the books are completely cataloged and classified by the Dewey decimal system. In the summer of 1945 a limited system of home loan secured by deposits was inaugurated. Both in Ponce and in San Juan the majority of the readers are school children.

The Carnegie Library of San Juan supplements the rather feeble work of the municipal library to some degree, but its position is

somewhat different owing to its historical background and its intended functions. It is supposed to be the insular library, and it
was known as such until July 27, 1916, when the new Carnegie
building was opened. It has developed a parcel-post delivery service, traveling libraries (or, rather, deposits subject to transfer), and
a few other attributes of a state library.[22] In reality, however, the
university library at Rio Piedras is far better qualified to serve as a
state (or national) library, and there is no reason why it could not
be operated in the same manner as the Oslo or Helsingfors university libraries, serving both the academic community and the island
as a whole.

The Carnegie Library's roots go back to 1899, the year after the
occupation of the island by the United States, when the collections of the Sociedad Económica de Amigos del País, the old
Spanish normal and professional schools, the former Intervención
de Hacienda y la Tesorería, the Diputación Provincial, and the
Instituto Civil de Segunda Enseñanza (closed soon thereafter) were
put together as the insular library. It was first known as the Biblioteca Pública Puertorriqueña or the San Juan Free Library, and it
was in the custody of the learned antiquarian Rudolph Adams van
Middeldyck. In March, 1903, this institution was formally con-
stituted as the Biblioteca Insular de Puerto Rico by an act of the
insular legislature; a board of trustees (junta de síndicos) was
created; the library was made a depository for insular government
publications; and a part of the library was designated as a circulating collection. The budget was increased, and the library prospered
under the administration of Don Manuel Fernández Juncos, the
vigorous interest of the great historian Dr. Cayetano Coll y Toste
(editor of the *Boletín histórico de Puerto Rico*), and the philan-
thropy of North American residents who knew and admired the
public library then coming into its own in the United States.

By 1913 the collection numbered twenty-five thousand volumes
together with valuable archives relating to Puerto Rican history.
By 1923 there were thirty thousand books in the library, but it is
significant that even then not all the rooms in the spacious new
building were devoted to the use of the library.[23] By the lat
1930's the collection exceeded the fifty thousand mark, and th
circulation amounted to some eighty-five thousand volumes an

nually.[24] Today there are some sixty-six thousand volumes in the library, but the annual report (unpublished except in sketchy excerpts in the annual report of the governor of Puerto Rico) for 1944—45 recorded a circulation of only 38,265 issues exclusive of the circulation of traveling libraries and the parcel-post service. Annual acquisitions were slightly under two thousand of which about a fourth was gift material. Over two hundred popular periodicals are currently received, of which 129 are in English, 78 in Spanish, 3 in French, and 2 in Portuguese. Fifteen daily papers from the United States, Mexico, Cuba, the Dominican Republic, Venezuela, Uruguay, and Argentina are available to readers. The traveling library program is limited by funds and equipment. Intended to stimulate group reading, it had 2,530 volumes in circulation in thirty diffcrent places in 1944—45. The parcel post service, intended for individuals rather than groups, calculated its services in 1944—45 in terms of 121 parcels holding a total of 392 books. Of course, in the case of both of these extramural services almost all the books circulated are in Spanish.

Another general collection of a semi-public character is the library of the Ateneo Puertorriqueño next door to the Carnegie Library in San Juan. The Ateneo, an institution for the promotion of popular culture by such activities as lectures and art exhibits, has a library of some two thousand uncataloged books, about six hundred of which are Puerto Rican items. The collection is intended to be a library of general literature with a few basic reference works. It receives some fifty popular magazines from all parts of North and South America, but only a few are bound. A full-time librarian is in charge, but he is handicapped by extremely limited funds.

The University of Puerto Rico Library at Rio Piedras, a half hour's drive through a continuous urban area from the center of San Juan, is by far the outstanding collection on the island, but it suffers from many handicaps, principally youth. This library cannot be said to have existed prior to 1924, inasmuch as between that date and the university's founding in 1903 the library was merely a neglected, uncataloged, amorphous collection which would have shamed a nineteenth-century American denominational college. During the twenty years prior to 1943, during which Mr. Dubois Mitchell was librarian, the collection grew from this embryonic state to that of a fairly good college library which gave reasonably adequate support to undergraduate instruction. Today it contains ninety-five thousand volumes, with ten to twenty thousand additional uncataloged items.

The university library is not a research library in any sense of the word. Its periodical collection is particularly weak (some three hundred and fifty are currently received, with relatively few complete sets), and the federal document collection is rather disorganized and incomplete owing to the lack of personnel trained to handle documents. Recent annual reports (typewritten only) show some rather slow progress in acquiring periodical sets, but, at the present rate, many student generations will pass before the university library has a periodical collection adequate even for the requirements of undergraduate term papers.

The collections cannot be described as strong in any field, not even in Spanish or Latin-American literature and history.[25] However, the Puerto Rican Collection is quite remarkable; and it was not without justification that the librarian stated in an informal report to the chancellor in 1943 that "the Puerto Rican Collection is the sole reason we have at the present time for graduate work." This collection is barely fifteen years old, and it was not opened officially until 1940.[26] Nevertheless, it contains almost twelve thousand books, among which are virtually all the important titles in the bibliography of Puerto Rico. It originated in 1929 when the university received a small donation of forty titles of Puerto Rican literary works. In the following year the books which were later to form the nucleus of the Puerto Rican Collection were separated from the rest of the library.

The first large-scale acquisition of Puerto Rican material was made in 1932, when the university purchased the private library of Sr. Vicente Rodríguez Rivera of Cayey, containing some six thousand volumes. In 1936 the university bought the exceptionally handsome collection of Puerto Rican books which had been brought together by Mr. Robert L. Junghanns of Bayamón. Mr. Junghanns, a New Yorker, was graduated from Cornell around the turn of the century and went to Puerto Rico with the intention of learning enough Spanish to permit him to conduct entomological investigations in South America. However, he became a permanent resident of the island and devoted much time to collecting insects, rocks, books, and periodicals. His library consisted of more than five thousand books, periodicals, pamphlets, and other material relative to the history of the island, and it was particularly strong in local newspapers and periodicals. When Pedreira, then head of the university's history department, died in 1939, his collection of about fifteen hundred carefully selected titles dealing with Puerto Rican history also passed to the library. The last important acquisition of Puerto Rican material was made in 1945, when the university purchased the admirable private library of the late Don Enrique Adsuar. Don Enrique had the means to acquire whatever he wanted, but he exercised great discrimination in the titles he admitted to his shelves, including such gems as Abbad y Lasierra's *Historia geográfica, civil y política de la isla de S. Juan Bautista de Puerto Rico* (Madrid, 1788) and the *Diario liberal y de variedades de Puerto Rico* (1821–22), the first daily newspaper on the island.

The Puerto Rican Collection of the university contains many other rare titles duplicated in few other collections. Such items as an anthology known as the *Aguinaldo Puerto-Riqueño* (San Juan, 1843)[27] and the long runs of the *Gaceta de Puerto Rico* (from 1812 to 1902, when it ceased publication) and the *Boletín mercantil de Puerto Rico* (1839–1918) offer the student of Puerto Rican history ample opportunity for research. At present the collection is housed in a special room which, although beautifully appointed, is entirely too small for it. Plans have been made to give it considerably more space in the new library building which is being contemplated.

During the war years the University of Puerto Rico, like the rest of the island, has enjoyed the most prosperous period in its history, thanks to the unprecedented revenues from rum taxes enjoyed by the insular government. That the library shared in this general prosperity is witnessed by the fact that a count of its collections in 1939 revealed 56,670 volumes, increasing to 66,995 in 1941, 74,054 in 1943, and 90,000 in 1944. Unfortunately, there is no reason to believe that the present prosperity will continue, and there have already been indications of a tendency to reduce appropriations for the university. The future financial position of the university library might possibly be improved somewhat if the library were given the functions and the prerogatives of a state or national library, thus justifying additional appropriations over and above the amounts allotted to it by the university from its total appropriation.

The University of Puerto Rico Library will probably never develop outstanding research collections in any field, but every effort should be made to strengthen the collections to a point where they will be adequate to support graduate work for a Master's degree in a few significant fields, such as Spanish philology and Latin-American history. In the foreseeable future it will be better for Puerto Rican aspirants for the doctorate to do their advanced study in North America rather than for the university to attempt to provide graduate study programs at home. The development of photographic facilities (at least microfilm readers) and the proposed new building for the university library, if its construction is actually realized, would contribute substantially to increasing the effectiveness of library service in Rio Piedras.

Special libraries in Puerto Rico have been rather weak until quite recently. Pedreira commented: "La falta de archivos, bibliotecas y museos que orienten con aportaciones iniciales la tarea del investigador ha sido una barrera formidable para ordenar y valorar nuestra inviolada producción literaria."[28] The first special library was a legal collection in San Juan established by royal order on June 19, 1831. This library subsequently became the property of the Puerto Rican Bar Association (Colegio de Abogados) and, after a brief sojourn during the 1930's in the university's law library, came to rest stored in boxes in the capitol building in San Juan. No officials of the Colegio de Abogados are familiar with the specific contents of this library, but it is said to have suffered heavily for losses due to constant moving and negligent borrowers of another generation.

The best legal library of Puerto Rico is the collection of the insular Supreme Court. Its beginnings can be traced back to 1912, and today it is said to hold some twenty thousand volumes, almost totally uncataloged except for some informal checking cards on the various reporting systems. There are fairly complete sets of nearly all federal reports, a large number of state reports, twelve complete law reviews, about five hundred textbooks, and some Spanish and British works, but nothing from other countries. An annual appropriation of $2,500 is available for the purchase of reports and books. There is no trained librarian, but the Puerto Rican insular marshal devotes some of his time to caring for the collection. While it is primarily for the reference use of the Supreme Court justices, it is also open to local attorneys for consultation and borrowing.

The library of the attorney-general of Puerto Rico is second in importance to that of the supreme court among legal collections of government agencies. It is only about fifteen years old, but it is reasonably complete in federal reports. It has a few state reports, a half-dozen law reviews in various states of completeness, and about a thousand textbooks and monographic works. Total holdings run to about ten thousand volumes. There is little older material and virtually nothing from outside the United States. The collection is fairly well cataloged, and it is available for consultation by local attorneys.

In 1944 and 1945 a vigorous campaign was conducted at the university to build up the law-school library. Prior to 1944 this collection contained only some forty-five hundred uncataloged volumes, was administered with extreme informality, and was subject only to the nominal jurisdiction of the university librarian. In order for the law school to be accredited and in order to provide adequate facilities for study, some seven thousand volumes were added in 1944–45, and the administrative conditions were radically changed. Today the university's law library is well cataloged, has a trained librarian in charge, and has an adequate budget for the purchase of current reports and law reviews. It has nearly all federal reports, state reports from forty-four states, and a representative collection of textbooks, including works by European authors. The few sets of law reviews are nearly all incomplete, but efforts are being made to fill them out.

At present it is being advocated that the libraries of the attorney-general and the supreme court be combined in one, to be housed in a proposed new Palacio de Justicia to be constructed in Muñoz Rivera Park in San Juan. Some local attorneys have even suggested that the University of Puerto Rico Law School be housed in this new legal center and that its library be incorporated with the other two. This proposal relative to the university's library was made prior to the rejuvenation of the law library at Rio Piedras, and today it might be more desirable to keep this collection separate, unless the law school itself is moved to the Palacio de Justicia. The combination of the supreme court library and the attorney-general's library would not only be an economical move but would also create a much stronger collection than either of the two component parts. Both are largely used at present by the same readers, members of the San Juan bar; and with the attorney-general and the supreme court under one roof, neither agency would suffer from losing its private library. It would be especially desirable from the standpoint of the Supreme Court's collection, since it would surely receive better care than is being given it at present.

Another library nominally connected with the University of Puerto Rico is the important collection of the School of Tropical Medicine in San Juan, sponsored jointly by Columbia University and the University of Puerto Rico as a research institute for investigation of tropical diseases and public health problems.[29] It is the only medical library of any consequence in the whole Caribbean area and probably the best one between New Orleans and Rio de Janeiro. Its beginnings may be traced to the old Instituto de Medicina Tropical, which was founded in 1905. When the School of Tropical Medicine was created in 1925, it took over the rather small library of the old Instituto. It is now well cataloged, and in recent years it has received fairly adequate financial support. Almost four hundred current journals in the various fields of medicine, chemistry, and biology are received. Complete sets of most of the more important American and British medical journals are available, but there are very few European periodicals. Total holdings amount to 3,885 monographic works and 6,742 volumes of periodicals. There are few academy or society publications. Some veterinary publications are included in the collection, but more valuable material in this field is available in the library of the Agricultural Experiment Station of the University of Puerto Rico near Rio Piedras. The library of the School of Tropical Medicine is open to the use of local physicians who obtain special permission from the director of the school.

In recent years there has been a good deal of discussion of the possibility of founding a medical school in Puerto Rico. The majority of medical opinion is against the project in as much as it is considered more economical to finance medical education of Puerto Ricans in North American universities. Unfortunately, the issue has become a political one, and in the course of the discussions that have taken place little thought has been given to the difficulty of building up adequate library, laboratory, and hospital facilities in centers far removed from San Juan. From the standpoint of securing adequate library service, it would seem to be most desirable to locate such a school close to the School of Tropical Medicine, but some have advocated that it be located far to the south in Ponce.

A second medical collection in San Juan is the library of the Department of Public Health. In 1940 Gropp estimated that it had 1,800 to 2,000 volumes and 156 periodical titles. At present this collection is boxed up and completely unavailable, and the librarian was unable to describe it adequately on account of the short period during which he has held office.

There are four agricultural libraries in Puerto Rico, and their administrative relations are most confusing. In the first place, it should be noted that the University of Puerto Rico, like the State System of Higher Education in Oregon or the Greater University of North Carolina, consists of two parts. The humanistic faculties and professional schools are in Rio Piedras, but the university's College of Agriculture and Mechanic Arts is in Mayagüez, a hundred miles (four hours by car) to the west. Nevertheless, the (insular government supported) Agricultural Experiment Station nominally attached to the College of Agriculture and Mechanic Arts is located in Rio Piedras on the other side of town from the university. The Federal Agricultural Experiment Station is in Mayagüez, but the Federal Forest Experiment Station is located in Rio Piedras in the same complex of buildings with the Insular Agricultural Experiment Station. Finally, the recently founded Instituto de Agricultura Tropical under the distinguished mycologist

Carlos E. Chardón is located in Mayagüez. It is supported by the insular government.

Starting in Rio Piedras, we find a fairly significant library in the Insular Agricultural Experiment Station (of the College of Agriculture and Mechanic Arts). The station library was begun as early as 1915, at which time a number of books had already been received and efforts were being made to establish exchange relationships with experiment stations in the continental United States, Latin America, and tropical regions in general.[30] In 1919 Director Edmundo D. Colón pushed the library project and secured a librarian whose duties also included supervision of the distribution of station publications. The hurricane of 1928 caused great damage to the library, and as a result of this disaster the collection was moved in 1930 into a fairly substantial structure remodeled to satisfy specific library needs. Until the summer of 1942 the library was uncataloged and unclassified in spite of the fact that it contained valuable sets of periodicals and other serials in agriculture and related fields. A recent count shows that the library holds 4,025 bound volumes, about 4,000 unbound volumes, and some 75,000 pamphlets. In addition to a large number of periodicals received by exchange, the library purchases 120 scientific journals by subscription. At present the total book fund is almost $5,000, of which $850 is set aside for subscriptions to periodicals.

Located in the same complex of buildings as the Insular Agricultural Experiment station is the federal Forest Experiment Station. Here there is a small working collection of about a thousand volumes on various aspects of forestry and forest economics, as well as a large number of forest experiment station bulletins. This collection is under the jurisdiction of the librarian of the United States Department of Agriculture.

Of the various libraries in Mayagüez the most important is that of the Federal Agricultural Experiment Station. This collection is also under the jurisdiction of the librarian of the United States Department of Agriculture. The library contains about twenty thousand volumes relating to agriculture and is in the custody of a full-time librarian employed under funds provided by the government of Puerto Rico at a salary of $1,800 a year. The books are classified according to the scheme used in the main library in Washington.

The fourth agricultural library in Puerto Rico, that of the Instituto de Agricultura Tropical, is only three years old but is growing rapidly. It is under the librarianship of Mr. José I. Otero, for many years the librarian of the Insular Agricultural Experiment Station in Rio Piedras. Between 1942 and 1945 the Instituto spent about $14,000 on books, which, when translated into terms of accessions, amounted to 4,573 volumes at the end of the fiscal year 1944—45. An annual appropriation of $410 is set aside for scientific periodicals, of which about sixty (exclusive of government documents) are currently received.[31].

The library of the College of Agriculture and Mechanic Arts resembles a liberal arts college library more than an agricultural library, although there is some emphasis on scientific publications. The college itself has never attained prestige in its field comparable to that of the faculties in Rio Piedras. As of 1945, the college library held 15,559 volumes, and new accessions were coming in at the approximate rate of a thousand volumes annually. There is little material of any value to research in any scientific field, but it is encouraging to note that in 1944—45 $3,600 was spent for completing periodical sets. At present the library maintains subscriptions to about 140 periodicals. The total budget for 1944—45 was $28,540—a considerable advance over previous years but still less than half of what was being spent on the humanistic and professional collections in Rio Piedras.[32]

In addition to the University of Puerto Rico and the College of Agriculture there are two other institutions of higher education in Puerto Rico—the Instituto Politécnico in San Germán and the Colegio del Sagrado Corazón, a Catholic girls' school, in Santurce, between San Juan and Rio Piedras. The misnamed Instituto Politécnico is actually a coeducational liberal arts college. Founded in 1912 as a private school, the Instituto inaugurated its college department in 1921. It is far smaller than the university, having only 319 students as against 3,508 in Rio Piedras and 780 in Mayagüez in 1944—45. The library contains 13,805 books, consisting largely of general works in the humanities and the sciences, with an attempt to approach as closely as possible the American standards for a liberal arts college library. Periodicals and most government documents are not accessioned. At present 139 periodicals are currently received by subscription. The library is not especially well supported, operating on a budget of $3,595.42 (1944–45), two-thirds of which is derived from student fees.

The only other college library in Puerto Rico is that of the Colegio del Sagrado Corazón, whose college department was founded in 1935. The library contains 13,250 volumes of a character similar to collections in North American Catholic girls' colleges. Some fifty periodicals of a general nature are received currently. It is the only library in Puerto Rico which separates its public card catalog into author-and-title and subject catalogs; and it is stated by the librarian that the practicality of this measure has been justified by more intelligent use of the library by students. Like the Instituto Politécnico, this library is largely supported by student fees.

The Insular Department of Education Library in San Juan is a fully cataloged collection of some four thousand titles of pedagogical content. Over fifty periodical titles are currently received. It is the only education library outside the university, and it is designed to serve teachers, principals, and school supervisors throughout the island. It is in the custody of a trained librarian.

There are said to be thirty-five high school libraries in Puerto Rico.[33] Most of them are neglected, uncataloged, and unread. The Office of Statistics of the Insular Department of Education in San Juan states that these thirty-five libraries contain 40,953 volumes in English and 40,834 in Spanish. Personal investigations of those which are alleged to be the best, Ponce and San Juan, reveal large numbers of duplicates (often ten or more copies of the same book) and a preponderance of textbooks over collateral and recreational reading. If any serious attempt is made to build up the school libraries in Puerto Rico, these collections will be of little value, even as a foundation.

During the war, libraries were established in Puerto Rico on the various military and naval reservations, but these are neither permanent installations nor are they devoted to the service of the people of Puerto Rico. There is a good chance that they will be converted into hospital libraries which the federal government will maintain for Puerto Rican veterans, even if the island becomes independent. At all events, these collections should not be removed from Puerto Rico; if they are not devoted to the service of the veterans, there is ample opportunity to put them to good use in the municipal libraries.

The deficiencies of Puerto Rican libraries are legion. Aside from poor financial support in normal times, the lack of professional interests among librarians and of co-operative projects is a significant factor in accounting for the weakness of the libraries. Puerto Rican librarians have no organizational activities —a matter all the more important because of difficulties involved in participating in conferences held in the United States. Badly needed projects such as a Puerto Rican union catalog, co-operative purchasing agreements, and improvement of extension services could be promoted by closer association of professional librarians.

Co-operation is needed particularly among the academic and special libraries. Elimination of duplication of effort and expenditure should be special goals of these libraries in view of the limited resources of the island, both in terms of finances and in terms of professional manpower available. For example, it might well prove to be impractical to alter the administrative or geographic position of the four agricultural libraries; but it would not be too big a job to draw up a union list of serials held by these libraries and to eliminate duplication of subscriptions to expensive scientific periodicals. By the same token, the establishment of a medical school in Ponce would necessitate an otherwise unjustified duplication of many expensive medical periodicals presently available in the library of the School of Tropical Medicine.

From the standpoint of popular libraries, the most effective measure would be an aggressive program undertaken by the insular government to bring library service to the hundreds of thousands of Puerto Ricans who do not now have access to books of any sort. At present Puerto Rico spends a relatively large proportion of the total governmental revenue on education.[34] Very little is devoted to libraries or, for that matter, to any other projects for continuing formal education. Outside of what is given to the Carnegie Library, nothing is appropriated to get books to the masses.

Puerto Rican educators might consider the advisability of establishing an insular service commission along the lines of North American state library commissions in some of our states with large rural populations. Before attempting to transplant North American methods, however, it would be well to give due consideration to specific characteristics of Puerto Rican popular culture, such as those described by Rodriguez Bou and Rogler. As a policy it might be most effective to concentrate on bringing libraries to the youth; for no matter how enthusiastic one may be for adult education, it is impossible to overlook the difficulties involved in making library readers of a people whose illiteracy rate is as high as it is in Puerto Rico. If a Puerto Rican library system is to be constructed with the primary goal of serving children and young people, it would possibly be best approached by reorganizing the high-school libraries to serve as public libraries in addition to their functions as school libraries.

The one dark side of the picture for the future of libraries in Puerto Rico is the immediate prospect of declining appropriations as the insular government's income from rum taxes decreases.The appropriations for the University of Puerto Rico have already been cut, and it will not be unreasonable to expect that those of other institutions will follow. On the other hand, Puerto Rico has today a larger number of trained technicians in all fields, including librarianship, than ever before. It is up to them to make up for any budgetary deficiencies by co-operative effort and by wise management of their own institutions.

Epilogue of 1970

This essay has been included in this collection on account of its historical perspective. It is gratifying to observe the substantial progress made in the last quarter of a century, to note the incorrect prognostication in the first sentence of the last paragraph, the correct one in the final sentence. The senior author of this article has not been on the island since the fall of 1945, and he earnestly hopes that this historical sketch can soon be brought up to date by a competent scholar.

62   Lawrence S. Thompson and Jorge Rivera Ruiz

NOTES

1. Writers' Program, Work Projects Administration, *Puerto Rico: A Guide to the Island of Borinquen* (New York: University Society, Inc., 1940), p. 122; Antonio S. Pedreira, *Curiosidades literarias de Puerto Rico* (San Juan: Biblioteca de autores puertorriqueños, 1939), p. 26. Pedreira's work is a compilation of literary anecdotes to accompany a prospectus of the publisher and also bears the title of *El Libro puertorriqucño.*

2. Writers' Program, *op. cit.,* p. 148.

3. Tomás Blanco, *Prontuario histórico de Puerto Rico,* 2d ed. (San Juan: Biblioteca de autores puertorriqueños, 1943), pp. 32-33; Angel Saavedra and Julio Fiol Negrón, *Historia de Puerto Rico* (San Juan, 1944), p. 22; Pedreira, *loc. cit.*

4. *Laurel de Apolo,* Silva II.

5. Pedreira, *loc. cit.*

6. Writers' Program, *op. cit.,* p. 122.

7. Luis O'Neill de Milán, "Bibliotecas públicas de Puerto Rico," in Eugenio Fernández García and Eugenio Astol (eds.), *El Libro de Puerto Rico* (San Juan: El Libro azul Publishing Co., 1923), p. 451.

8. *Ibid.*

9. "Tentativa del Prebendado Dr. D. Rufo Manuel Fernández de fundar en la capital una biblioteca pública," *Boletín Histórico de Puerto Rico,* X (1923), 62.

10. I (1863), 19-24. There is a copy of this extremely rare periodical in the private library of Professor Rafael W. Ramirez de Arellano of Rio Piedras. Professor Ramirez is Asenjo's grandson.

11. Writers' Program, *op. cit.,* p. 122.

12. Emilio del Toro Cuevas, "Influencia de la biblioteca pública moderna en la familia y en la cultura social," *Conferencias dominicales dadas en la Biblioteca Insular de Puerto Rico,* I (1913), 52; Manuel Fernández Juncos, "Bibliotecas públicas de Puerto Rico," *Conferencias dominicales dadas en la Biblioteca Insular de Puerto Rico,* I (1913), 122, and "Bibliotecas antillanas: Puerto Rico," *Revista de las Antillas: Magazine hispano-americano,* I (May, 1913), 39. (The two articles by Fernández Juncos are almost identical.) The Writers' Program is in error when it states (*op. cit.,* p. 123) that the Mayagüez Municipal Library was founded in 1875.

13. Fernández Juncos, "Bibliotecas públicas de Puerto Rico," p. 133, and "Bibliotecas antillanas: Puerto Rico," p. 37.

14. Pedreira, *op. cit.,* p. 42.

15. But Fernández Juncos counted only 3,235 and 3,181 volumes respectively in his two articles written in 1913.

16. Del Toro Cuevas, *op. cit.,* p. 52; O'Neill de Milán, *op. cit.,* p. 451.

17. Fernández Juncos, "Bibliotecas públicas de Puerto Rico," pp. 134-35. M. G. Nin, supervising principal of public schools in the Yauco District, was said to have been the moving spirit behind this project.

18. Arthur E. Gropp, *Guide to Libraries and Archives in Central America and the West Indies, Panama, Bermuda, and British Guiana* ("Middle American Research Series," No. 10) (New Orleans: Middle American Research Institute, Tulane University of Louisiana, 1941), pp. 612-36.

19. *El Analfabetismo en Puerto Rico* (Rio Piedras: University of Puerto Rico, Consejo Superior de Enseñanza, 1945), p. 53. A large proportion of Puerto Rico's illiterates are undoubtedly adults, but the exact figure is not available.

20. *Comerío: A Study of a Puerto Rican Town* ("Social Science Series") (Lawrence: University of Kansas, 1940), p. 177.

21. *Insularismo: Ensayos de interpretación puertorriqueña*, 2d ed. (San Juan: Biblioteca de autores puertorriqueños, 1942), p. 109.

22. Writers' Program, *op. cit.*, p. 215.

23. O'Neill de Milán, *op. cit.*, p. 451.

24. Writers' Program, *op. cit.*, p. 215.

25. The library of the Instituto Ibero-Americano reported by Gropp has been absorbed by the university library.

26. Data on the Puerto Rican Collection have been furnished by Sr. Gonzalo Velazquez, associate librarian at the university, who has devoted much time and energy to building it up.

27. Until recently supposed to be the first book (not item) published in Puerto Rico. However, a few years ago, a title by Fray Manuel María de San Lucar, *Quadernito de varias especies de coplas muy devotas* ("Impreso en Puerto Rico, año de 1812. En 8°"), was discovered in a 1924 catalog issued by Victorio Vindel, a Madrid dealer. Vindel was unable to remember to whom the book was sold, and no copy has been located thus far. If the 1812 date is correct, the Capuchin missionary San Lucar will enjoy the honor of being the first person to write a book published in Puerto Rico.

28. *Insularismo*, p. 52.

29. A short description of this library appears in Columbia University, *Announcement of the School of Tropical Medicine of the University of Puerto Rico, Twentieth Session, 1945-46*, p. 12.

30. Melville T. Cook and José I. Otero, "History of the First Quarter of a Century of the Agricultural Experiment Station at Rio Piedras, Puerto Rico," in Puerto Rico University, College of Agriculture and Mechanic Arts, Agricultural Experiment Station, *Bulletin*, XLIV (1937), 94-99.

31. The growth of the library may be traced by referring to Puerto Rico, Instituto de Agricultura Tropical, *Informe anual del director, 1942-43*, pp. 10-12, and *Informe anual del director, 1943-44*, pp. 10-12, with illustrations of the premises.

32. Unpublished report for 1943-44 of the library of the College of Agriculture and Mechanic Arts, Puerto Rico University.

33. Gropp, *op. cit.*, reported twenty-four high school libraries, and other figures are available in the annual reports of the insular commissioner of education. The hurricanes have been particularly vicious enemies of books in Puerto Rican high-school libraries. Mr. Thomas S. Hayes, librarian of the University of Puerto Rico, states that when he went to Humacao as principal of the high school in 1927, he found an excellent although uncataloged collection of some six thousand titles. The entire library, was completely destroyed in the hurricane of 1928.

34. According to Writers' Program, *op. cit.*, p. 125, about one-third of the total governmental revenue was spent on education in "normal" times prior to World War II.

Library Development
In the English-Speaking West Indies[*]

To a librarian who has visited the West Indies in 1938, 1944—45, 1950, and 1953, it is apparent that striking changes have taken place in the last two decades.[1] For three centuries the West Indies have gone without books, but today the some 3,000,000 souls in the English-speaking islands of the eastern and western Caribbean have entered a new era of library service. Over two hundred years ago a traveller in the West Indies was annoyed by the philistine, anti-intellectual attitude of the colonials,[2] contrasting unfavorably with the North American continent, where a half a dozen colleges and numerous libraries were already flourishing. In 1823 John Stewart commented disparagingly on Jamaicans: "Nine-tenths of the inhabitants never think of reading anything beyond a news-paper, business and pleasure engrossing too much of their atten-tion to leave much leisure for reading."[3] Just before World War II a Royal Commission which inquired into the nature of the riots of 1937 and 1938 placed a large proportion of the blame on il-literacy, inadequate schools, and deficient library service.

The public library movement in the English-speaking Caribbean is roughly contemporary with similar events in old and New Eng-land. Indeed, the Bridgetown Public Library was founded on the basis of the Barbados Public Library Act of 21 October 1847, legislation which antedated a similar enactment in the United Kingdom by three years.[4] Around the turn of the century

*Reprinted with permission of the publisher from *Libri*,v (1955), 256-266.

Carnegie libraries were established in many localities, but they were not given proper support, were allowed to run down, and frequently were converted into subscription libraries as the polilla and the cockroach fattened on the bookstock. In 1933 Ernest A. Savage was requested by the Carnegie Corporation of New York to investigate library conditions in the West Indies, and he produced the important report entitled *Libraries of Bermuda, the Bahamas, the British West Indies, British Guiana, British Honduras, Puerto Rico, and the American Virgin Islands.*[5] This investigation was followed in 1941 by Arthur E. Gropp's *Guide to Libraries and Archives in Central America and the West Indies, Panama, Bermuda, and British Guiana, Supplemented with Information on Private Libraries, Bookbinding, Bookselling, and Printing,*[6] the result of an extensive survey sponsored by the Rockefeller Foundation in 1937 and 1938. The two basic surveys had their effect, and in 1941 the first evidence of it was seen in the launching of the Central Library Scheme for Trinidad and Tobago under the unusually competent supervision of an experienced Canadian librarian, Helen Gordon Stewart. It was financed by a $70,000 grant from the Carnegie Corporation. It is unfortunate that the program had to be initiated at such an inauspicious date, and it is only through competent management that it survived at all during the lean wartime years.

Two other important surveys were still to be conducted at the end of the war. Nora Bateson's *Library Plan for Jamaica*[7] offered an intelligent, carefully-thought-out proposal for adequate library service to the nearly million and a half people on this largest Caribbean island inhabited by an English-speaking population. Rodolfo O. Rivera's *A Program of Public Libraries for Puerto Rico*[8] is significant only indirectly for the other non-self-governing territories; for Puerto Rico, as a result of her actual and potential natural and economic resources, has developed more rapidly than any of the other islands and is considered a model of progress in the Caribbean. Rivera recommended that sums well into seven figures be spent on public library development in Puerto Rico, a program of a magnitude that could only be partially matched even by Jamaica and Trinidad, the two largest English-speaking islands. N. G. Fisher revealed quite pointedly in a report on the "Library

Aspects of the Caribbean Seminar[9] that the financial limitations of the English-speaking islands would hamper library development gravely and that outside financial help is almost a prerequisite.

Higher education has developed very slowly in the English-speaking West Indies. Codrington College in Bridgetown has its origins in the early eighteenth century; and while its influence has been steady and not insignificant over the last two centuries, especially after it assumed university rank upon affilation with the University of Durham in 1875, its student body and teaching staff are small and its course offerings restricted to a theological curriculum and some classical studies. Its main building was gutted with fire in April, 1926. In 1921 the Imperial College of Tropical Agriculture[10] was founded on the basis of recommendations from a committee appointed by the late Lord Milner when he was secretary of state for colonies in 1919. It received help from many sources, including a $5,000 grant from the Carnegie Corporation for the library. Today the collections total some 19,000 bound volumes, 22,000 unbound volumes, and 39,000 unbound parts of periodicals, representing perhaps the most significant specialized collection on tropical agriculture anywhere in the world.

Unfortunately, neither Codrington College nor the Imperial College of Tropical Agriculture were in a position or in any sense obligated to lend leadership to the West Indian library movement. It was not until 1946 that a general higher institution, the University College of the West Indies, was founded, and its buildings, including a small but well planned library (opened May, 1952) have all been erected since October, 1948, near Kingston, Jamaica.[11] In 1953 the library's collections amounted to 22,918 volumes, 3,256 pamphlets, 158 maps, 152 microfilms and filmstrips, 70,590 parts of periodicals, 13,876 government serials, and 563 calendars; and the acquisition statistics could show 374 exchanges for such valuable publications as the *Caribbean Quarterly*, *Caribbean Affairs Pamphlets* the *West Indian Medical Journal, Social and Economic Studies,* and the *Current Caribbean Bibliography* (published jointly with the Caribbean Commission, *infra*).[12] While it would be doubtful whether N. G. Fisher's suggestion that a regular school of librarianship be founded here has any merit at present (and the same comment applies to a similar suggestion by Rodolfo Rivera for the University of Puerto Rico), tutorial work within the framework of the examination system of the British Library Association is well adapted to the needs of library training in such situations as the West Indies present; and such instruction has been given successfully at the University College. But perhaps the most important factor of all is that the University College of the West Indies, like the University of Puerto Rico (including the branches in Rio Piedras and Mayagüez), is a potential research center from which studies in all fields bearing on West Indian librarianship may be conducted and from which leaders, both librarians and non-librarians, may emerge to promote the cause of more and better reading in the islands.

In addition to the surveys of conditions for public library development and the rise of higher education, two independent agencies are of considerable importance for librarianship in the West Indies, one on a local basis and one on a regional basis. The Institute of Jamaica, created by Law 22 of 1879 "to establish and maintain an institution comprising a library, reading rooms and museum . . ." among other purposes, has developed certain very significant library services over the years.[13] Under the librarianship of Frank Cundall from 1891 to 1937 an unusually handsome collection of West Indiana was built, now containing over 17,000 items and rivalled only by the Puerto Rican Collection of the University of Puerto Rico in its field.[14] In addition, however, the Institute has a science library (about 7,000 volumes), a general library with nearly 30,000 volumes, and two junior centers which serve some 5,000 children between ten and eighteen. *The Handbook of Jamaica* reports that the general library of the Institute will ultimately be added to the Headquarters Library of the Jamaica Library Service to form a Central Lending Library for Kingston and St. Andrew.

The other important independent agency for library development in the West Indies is the Caribbean Commission and its library in Port-of-Spain, Trinidad.[15] This four-power agency is operated jointly by the four metropolitan countries which control the non-self-governing territories of the Caribbean (the United States, Great Britain, France, and the Netherlands). Research is conducted on a regional basis in all aspects of the social and economic life of the jurisdictions concerned. There are several important publications with the Caribbean Commission imprint, of which we may note the *Yearbook of Caribbean Research,* the *Caribbean Commission Monthly Information Bulletin,* the *Caribbean Economic Review,* the summary reports of the West Indian Conferences, the annual reports of the Commission, and special bulletins in West Indian agriculture, economics, sociology, and related subjects. The library is relatively small, but it is reasonably comprehensive in recent books, periodicals, and official documents relative to the territories it serves. The latter collection is extremely important, since the national libraries of the various metropolitan governments have had some difficulty in securing West Indian documents. At the time this writer surveyed the Caribbean Commission Library in October-November 1953 he suggested that it might be advisable for each jurisdiction served by the Commission to draw up depository legislation whereby the Caribbean Commission Library would receive enough copies of each colonial document to place one in each of the national libraries and the major research libraries of the Netherlands, France, Great Britain, and the United States. In 1953 the library contained about 2,300 well selected books and perhaps four times that number of documents and loose serials. With the resources of the library of the Imperial College of Tropical Agriculture in nearby St. Augustine, the Eastern Caribbean Regional Library, the Trinidad Public Library, and the small collection of law books and local public documents in the Supreme Court Library at the Red House (government building) in Port-of-Spain, the Caribbean Commission Library can afford to continue its selective policy. Especially important is the library staff's aggressive interest in regional bibliography (e.g., *Current Caribbean Bibliography*) and all aspects of librarianship not only in Trinidad but also in the entire Caribbean.

With this stage-setting of library development, past and present, in the English-speaking Caribbean, we are in a position to understand the background and future possibilities for library service. In 1941 Helen Gordon Stewart undertook a project which would have been difficult in peace time and was all but impossible in wartime.[16] Her work was the basis for what is known today as the Trinidad and Tobago Central Library, an agency that circulates over 150,000 books annually to nearly 20,000 readers outside of Port-of-Spain.

Savage and the Carnegie Corporation had definite plans for extending library service to the smaller islands in the Eastern Caribbean, and Carnegie had even planned to grant $10,000 for this purpose. Extension of service was envisioned through a scheme of circulating boxes of books to the other islands. However, Carnegie's policy changed in the meanwhile, and the $10,000 was never granted. Moreover, it was realized that the box-of-books idea was not very practical. At this point the British Council entered the picture; and on 1 January 1945 it began to finance the program of setting up demonstration libraries on each island, supported by a regional central library (the East Caribbean Regional Library), and subsequently handing the libraries over to the local governments.[17] The last was, of course, conditional upon the willingness and ability of the local governments to support free public libraries.

One of the gravest obstacles to library development in the Caribbean is the paradoxical fact that public libraries already existed. However, in most instances the existing Carnegie library established in the early part of the century had been compelled to charge a subscription in order to keep it open at all, for most of the islands are too poor to finance education and libraries independently of outside aid. Bridgetown and Port-of-Spain are notable exceptions. The public library in the former community had been a free tax-supported institution for a century and was circulating well over a quarter of a million books annually from its stock of more than 50,000 volumes. It had a competent staff to serve some 20,000 borrowers, and it was even able to open an attractive branch at Speightstown in 1949. Still the Regional Library could give help through the presentation of urgently needed books and the training of a member of the staff for the Library Association's entrance examination.[18] The Trinidad Public Library in Port-of-Spain was founded in 1851 and was supported through ordinance-established grants from the government and the city council; but precisely one hundred years after its foundation, the Trinidad Public Library made its fine collections of more than 60,000 volumes and services available without charge to all citizens of the community. There is no jurisdictional conflict with the Trinidad and Tobago Central Library, which scrupulously restricts itself to service outside of Port-of-Spain. The only other non-subscription libraries in the region in 1945 were the Public Library in Road Town, Tortola, British Virgin Islands, and the Georgetown, British Guiana, Public Library.

Thus the first step was to set up demonstration projects wherever there was no free public library service. Ordinarily a collection of two or three thousand books was placed in an existing building, necessary new furniture provided, and a local librarian trained to handle the circulation. These simple demonstrations had a striking effect, and the next stage was soon reached, when local authorities recognized their responsibility for providing free public library service and took over the books and equipment. The Regional Library would continue to add essential material to the collections the next few years and provide staff training. The results speak for themselves: Five subscription libraries, Grenada, St. Kitts-Nevis, St. Vincent, St. Lucia, and Antigua, had accepted the principle of free public library service under the stimulus of the demonstration projects. Despite the comment by local officials in Dominica that the demonstration "holds much promise for cultural development,"[19] the project at Roseau had to be abandoned for lack of support.

The most northerly islands in the Leewards, the British Virgins, represented a special problem, for their economy is closely linked with that of the nearby American Virgins (Danish prior to 1917). A free public library was established at Road Town, Tortola, in 1942. The Regional Library felt some doubt that adequate service could ever be provided on such small, remote islands, with meagre finances, but steps were nevertheless taken to lend some assistance in the way of training personnel. At the same time the Tortola Library was assisted with books and professional advice from the nearby St. Thomas Public Library at Charlotte Amalie in the American Virgins, a well organized and well administered library on the continental American model with reasonably good finances, a collection of 20,000 volumes (including some West Indiana), and even a branch on tiny St. John. Together with the public libraries on St. Croix at Christiansted and Frederiksted, collections of public library books in the American Virgins total over 30,000 volumes. Close ties with the British Virgins in educational and general social services would seem to be highly desirable insofar as they are administratively feasible.

Brief mention might be made of British Guiana, where a comparatively strong free public library has existed at Georgetown since its establishment by a Carnegie grant in 1909. With the help of the Regional Library six additional book centers in the immediate hinterland of Georgetown were established in 1950 with high hope of success under the direction of the Georgetown Public Library.

From the local standpoint a typical case may be seen in St. Vincent. A library existing since 1888 in Kingston was reestablished in 1907 when a Carnegie building was provided, and in 1947 the Regional Library demonstration project was initiated. By 1951 there were branches at Georgetown, Calliqua, Barrouallie, and Layou and a deposit station at Bequia. Law no. 4 of 1950 made the government solely responsible for library service, removing all burdens from the municipal bodies. It was stated by local officials that "The linking of the library with the Eastern Caribbean Regional Library has been the means of placing at the disposal of readers books which cannot be obtained in the local library," but other benefits were also recognized.[20]

Grenada offers another opportunity for observing a West Indian library situation at close range through Martha Louise Pitt's *Survey of Libraries in Grenada, B.W.I.*[21] A public library has existed in St. George since 1846, and in 1892 it was transferred to its present quarters, a well-ventilated, well-lighted second floor of a warehouse. Under the stimulus of the regional project, the library abandoned subscriptions and became free in 1949. Demonstration work had been carried on from 1947 to 1949 when the government accepted the responsibility for providing funds to continue the project on a permanent basis. A trained librarian was employed, a third of the original bookstock of 12,000 volumes discarded and an additional 1,500 sent to bindery, recataloging was undertaken with substantial help from the headquarters library, and some 4,500 volumes (a third of them juveniles) from the demonstration project were accessioned with a record of their origin. There is an assistant librarian, a children's librarian, and two junior assistants. There is what amounts to a branch on the large island of Carriacou and four rural book centers as of 1949.

The largest library in the regional scheme is the Trinidad and Tobago Central Library.[22] It was formally taken over by the government of the colony in 1949, and it has subsequently increased its services and bookstock substantially. In 1952 there were seventy-six different service points, including two regional branches (San Fernando in southern Trinidad and Scarborough in Tobago), seven branch libraries, sixty-five book centers, one deposit collection at the Imperial College of Tropical Agriculture, and, of course, the headquarters collection. Most significant, perhaps, has been the rejuvenation of the Carnegie Free Library in San Fernando under a system of voluntary cooperation with the Central Library. Since 1948, when the cooperation began, circulation at San Fernando has increased from 6,000 to 108,000 in 1952. An especially gratifying note is the marked increase in children's reading.

The Trinidad and Tobago Central Library has been unusually effective, thanks in part to the comparatively favorable financial position of this colony and thanks in part to imaginative and adaptible administration. For example, the bookmobile, which enjoys such great favor in western Europe and North America, is less practical on most of the islands, with poor roads and communication systems, than in established book centers. As a result, rotating collections have been established in many villages, and the people have begun to look on such small libraries as a permanent aspect of community life.[23]

One of the most important features of the Regional Library is a union catalog of the collections in the various libraries within the system. It is possible to exchange books between the various collections with little formality and only a minimum of record keeping. Another significant aspect of Regional Library's work is the practical training program. Based on the examination system of the British Library Association, the first six-months course was held from January to June, 1949, and both this and subsequent courses have proven their worth in preparing young librarians for examinations.

Jamaica presents entirely different problems of library service because of its size and potential wealth and because of the presence near Kingston of the University College of the West Indies. Since the late thirties there has been something of a cultural and political renaissance in Jamaica, and not only libraries but also other aspects of community life have made noteworthy advances. Especially important was the inauguration of a new constitution late in 1944 after seventy-eight years without one.

When the Bateson report was submitted in 1945, there were or had been four parish public libraries. The Manchester Free Library in Mandeville, opened in April, 1938, is the first free public library on the island, and since January, 1944, it has had a trained librarian. The British Council made substantial contributions toward the cataloging of the Manchester Library and other aspects of its organization. The Saint Elizabeth Public Library was founded in 1944 and held well over 2,000 books in 1950. The St. James Public Library at Montego Bay opened in June, 1945. In Port Antonio a small collection for the Portland Parish was established in August, 1943, with some slight aid from the British Council, but unfortunately the books were washed away in a violent storm exactly a year later. Outside of the Institute of Jamaica, the only other library of any consequence on the island was the collection of some 2,000 volumes in the Department of Agriculture at Hope.

By Jamaica Law no. 62 of 1949 an island-wide library service was established. It is controlled by the Jamaica Library Board, consisting of the director of libraries (chairman), the minister of education, and representatives appointed by the University College of the West Indies, the board of governors of the Institute of Jamaica, and the Parochial Boards' Association. There is a Headquarters Library which includes not only a core collection but also a student collection for direct postal loans, a small West Indies collection, and a drama collection consisting of plays available for loan to organizations. Nine communities now have parish libraries, and only five of the fourteen parishes on the island do not have libraries. There are five branch libraries and a number of book centers.

In 1950 the Jamaica Library Board recommended the appropriation of special funds for school libraries, but the government was unable to provide help. However, the Board did offer help by drawing up a list of books for school libraries and maintaining a supply of these titles, fully processed and ready for incorporation into school libraries for those schools which could pay the list prices. This move was in line with the Bateson recommendation, which urged that elementary schools be helped to spend the very modest maximum of £ 6 annually allowed by the government for library books for each school.

The English-speaking West Indies offer an unusual case study in the provision of library service to underdeveloped, geographically remote regions in which very limited public funds are available for library service. It has taken two full decades since the Savage report to get effective programs of library service under way, although allowance must be made for the difficulties of accomplishing much in war time. The imported leaders have shown great perseverance, ingenuity, and devotion in working to attain their stated objectives. Much outside help has been given, and some may always be necessary for the very small islands. However, the local governments have awakened to their responsibility to provide free library service. Still, all outside help should not be cut off precipitously simply because of the rather spectacular initial success. With the growing number of native West Indians trained as librarians, and with the increasingly favorable attitude of authorities toward expansion of free library service, the prospects for cultural development in the English-speaking Caribbean are more favorable than at any previous time in the last three centuries.

NOTES

1. This essay will cover only the non-self-governing, English-speaking islands of the Caribbean. Bermuda and the Bahamas, too remote geographically to form a unit with Jamaica and the eastern Caribbean, have been omitted. On Puerto Rico see Lawrence S. Thompson and Jorge Rivera Ruiz, "The Libraries of Puerto Rico," *Library Quarterly*, XVI (1946), 225-238. For general background on educational conditions in the British West Indies see Great Britain, Colonial Office, Education Commission, *Education in the Windward and Leeward Islands* (London, H.M.S.O., 1939; "Colonial no. 164").

2. "A New Library Service: Caribbean Developments," *Times Educational Supplement*, no. 1642 (19 October 1946), p. 504.

3. *A View of the Past and Present State of the Island of Jamaica; with Remarks on the Moral and Physical Condition of the Slaves, and on the Abolition of Slavery in the Colonies* (Edinburgh, Oliver and Boyd, 1823), p. 204.

4. Great Britain, Colonial Office, *Annual Report for Barbados*, 1947 (1948), p. 33. The Colonial Office annual reports are rather uneven in their treatment of library activities.

5. London, The Library Association, 1934.

6. New Orleans, Middle American Research Institute, Tulane University, 1941 ("Middle American Research Series," no. 10). See also Mrs. Dorothy M. Gropp, "Vignettes of Libraries and Archives in the West Indies," *Louisiana Library Association Bulletin*, II (December, 1938), 5-9, and *ibid.* (March, 1939), 3-6.

7. Kingston, Government Printer, 1945. See also her essay, "Today, the Minds of Men," *Library Journal*, LXX (1 November 1945), 997-999.

8. San Juan de Puerto Rico, Committee on Design of Public Works, December, 1946.

9. *Manchester Review*, VI (1953), 429-431.

10. A good general account of the founding and early years may be found in Algernon Aspinall, *A Wayfarer in the West Indies* (Boston, Houghton Mifflin, 1931), pp. 81-84.

11. Harold Holdsworth, "University College of the West Indies Library," *Library Association Record*, LV (1953), 278-281, and F. L. Kent, "University and Research Library Notes," *ibid.*, LIV (1952), 63.

12. Statistics of library holdings from *The Yearbook of the Universities of the Commonwealth*, XXXI (1954), 1476.

13. *The Handbook of Jamaica*, LXI (1951), 522 *et seq.*, and Great Britain, Colonial Office, *Report on Jamaica*, 1951 (1953), p. 128 *et seq.*

14. Gonzalo Velázquez, "Pride of the University; Puerto Rican Collection Has Many Rarities," *Library Journal*, LXX (1946), 453-454. Although even the very small libraries in the English-speaking islands have been unusually aware of the significance of local history, only one other collection, that of the Trinidad Public Library in Port-of-Spain, has a major scholarly significance.

15. Bernard L. Poole, *The Caribbean Commission; Background of Cooperation in the West Indies* (Columbia, University of South Carolina Press, 1951) and Willis Grafton Nealley, *The Caribbean Commission as an International Instrument for Regional Collaboration* (unpublished Ph. D. dissertation, Stanford University, 1947).

16. Helen Gordon Stewart, "Regional Library of the Eastern Caribbean," *Pacific Northwest Library Association Quarterly*, XIV (October, 1949), 27-30.

17. Eastern Caribbean Regional Library, *ECRL, a Regional Experiment; a Report on the progress of the Eastern Caribbean Regional Library, 1941-9150* (Port-of-Spain, 1951) and David Karl Easton, "Public Library Service in the

British Territories of the Eastern Caribbean," *UNESCO Bulletin for Libraries,* V (1951), 421-426.

18. Great Britain, Colonial Office, *Annual Report for Barbados,* 1949 (1950), p. 30.

19. Great Britain, Colonial Office, *Annual Report for Dominica,* 1947 (1949), p. 31.

20. Great Britain, Colonial Office, *Annual Report for St. Vincent,* 1950 and 1951 (1953), pp. 26-28.

21. Unpublished master's essay (M.S. in L.S.), Catholic University of America, 1951.

22. An extended *Annual Report* has been issued for the past five years. Reports on the San Fernando Carnegie Free Library are also included.

23. Jack Smeaton, "Books Vans or Book Centres? Rural Library Service in the West Indies," *Library Association Record,* LIV (1952), 195-198.

The First Non-Serial
Puerto Rican Imprint *

While the first printing in Puerto Rico began with the *Gàceta de Puerto Rico* in 1808 or earlier, there has been some question as to when the first non-serial Puerto Rican imprint appeared. For some time it was believed that 1812 was the date of the first such imprint. Antonio S. Pedreira, who heard of a great deal more than he ever saw, mentions two such works in his *Bibliografía puertorriqueña*, both with extremely meagre descriptions, *viz.*, (1) Manuel María Sanlúcar: *Sermón, 2 de mayo de 1812*. P.R., 1812. 18 p. and (2) José María Santaella: *Discurso panegírico que hizo a sus feligreses*. P.R., 1812. 18 p. A third 1812 imprint was noted in "Catálogo Número 1" of the Librería de Victoria Vindel, Relatores 2, Madrid, in 1924, *viz.*, San Lucar, Fray Manuel María de. (Misionero Capuchino) *Quadernito de varias especies de coplas muy devotas. Impreso en Puerto Rico, año de 1812*. En 8°; Cuero azul filetes, bandas interiores, cortes dorados. 350 pesetas. No copy of the two pamphlets by Sanlúcar or of the one by Santaella has ever been located.

Recently the William L. Clements Library acquired the following: D. ANTONIO IGNACIO DE CORTABARRIA, | CABALLERO PENSIONADO DE LA REAL Y DISTINGUIDA ORDEN | ESPAÑOLA DE CARLOS III.°, MINISTRO TOGADO DEL REAL Y | SUPREMO CONSEJO DE CASTILLA, Y COMISIONADO REGIO PARA LA | PACIFICACION GENERAL DE LAS PROVINCIAS DE VENEZUELA. | *A los vecinos y habitantes de las Provincias de* |

*Reprinted with permission of the publisher from 'Papers of the Bibliographical Society of America', XLIV (1950), 181-182.

Caracas, Barinas, Cumaná, y Nueva Barcelona. [1]-[8] p., of which p. [8] is blank. 30 x 20½ cm. "Puerto-Rico 20 de Julio de 1811" (p. 7). Rebound in one-quarter dark-green oasis niger. Spine title: CORTABARRIA. PROCLAMA A LOS VECINOS Y HABITANTES DE LAS PROVINCIAS DE CARACAS ETC.—PUETO [*sic*] RICO 1811.

A related pamphlet has been located in the Yale University Library: D. ANTONIO IGNACIO DE CORTABARRIA, | CABALLERO PENSIONADO DE LA REAL Y | DISTINGUIDA ORDEN ESPAÑOLA DE CARLOS III.°, | MINISTRO TOGADO DEL REAL Y SUPREMO CON- | SEJO DE CASTILLA, Y COMISIONADO REGO PARA | LA PACIFICACION GENERAL DE LAS PROVINCIAS | DE VENEZUELA. | *Á los Pueblos de las Provincias de* | *Caracas, Barinas, Cumaná, y Nueva* | *Barcelona.* 1. [1]-[60] p., 1. P. [60] is blank. 13½ x 19¼ cm. "Puerto-Rico 20 de setiembre de 1811" (p. 59). In green, black, and white stenciled paper cover.

PART THREE

BOOKBINDING

Introductory Notes on the History of
Bookbinding in Spanish America[*]

A comprehensive view of any aspect of the history of Spanish America is considerably more difficult than a comparable study dealing with the English-speaking peoples of North America. The lack of political unity, the relatively low economic standards, the vast distances and poor communication systems (only partially overcome even today by airplane and radio), and, above all, the wide diffusion of source materials have combined to make the tasks of Latin Americanists unusually difficult.

In making this preliminary survey of the history of hand binding in Spanish America, the writer has encountered more problems than in any one of half a dozen other studies of the history of books and libraries in the Americas south of Miami and the Rio Bravo del Norte. It has been necessary to excavate undocumented notes from general histories and imprint bibliographies, to conduct extensive (and frequently ignored) correspondence with libraries, archives, and binders' ateliers, and to pick the brains of fellow bibliophiles. The response of the latter has been by far the most rewarding source; for modern Latin America, with its relative freedom from predatory internal revenue agencies, has produced a significant and creative generation of collectors. For these reasons, most of the source material on which this essay is based is in the form of notes and correspondence now in the Division of Special Collections, Margaret I. King Library, University of Kentucky.

*Reprinted with permission of the publisher from *Libri,* x (1960), 10-22.

The *Urgeschichte* of bookbinding in Spanish America, extends to the pre-Columbian period[1]. Some twenty examples of Mayan and Aztec books, written, rather painted, in hieroglyphic forms in the fifteenth and sixteenth centuries, have survived in libraries of Mexico and Europe. The writing material of non-animal origin was probably the fibrous inner bark of some species of wild fig (*amatl*, or paper tree), not the product of the *maguey* (century plant), a statement frequently found in earlier descriptions of these books. Those on animal hides vaguely resemble parchment in that the skins have been scraped thin and dressed with chalk. Whether on bark paper or skin, the same type of "binding" was used. The first leaf was painted on the verso only, the second on the recto only, and the two were attached at the inner margin. The third leaf again was painted on the verso, the fourth on the recto, and so on; but the second leaf was joined to the third at the outer margin, the third to the fourth at the inner margin, and so on to form a continuous strip when laid out end to end, but capable of being folded into a codex book. The books on bark paper were likely to be glued together at the appropriate margins, while those on skins were attached with leather thongs. The late Nathan van Patten speculated that the form of the pre-Columbian Middle American book may have originated under an Asiatic, specifically Chinese, influence; but he offers no more concrete evidence than does Miss van Regemorter in her recent suggestion that the European codex may have originated in something that looks like a book in the hands of figures on Hittite steles[3]. Indeed, if we actually knew what was originally in the "binders' boards" for the earliest Egyptian books[4], the pseudo-historians who associate the pre-Conquest Middle Americans with the peoples of the Nile and even with the Lost Tribes might have still less damp powder and soft shot for their unscholarly blunderbusses. The story of binding can be told only on the basis of physical evidence, and all speculation must be ruled out.

The *conquistadores* did an effective job of destroying most aspects of Amerind culture excepting that *versunkenes Kulturgut* which survives as well-nigh indestructible folk art. Books are not among objects produced by folk artists in Spanish America. However, there was a curious sort of a compromise between the Aztec codex and the European book during the first half century after the conquest of Mexico. Generally produced on *amatl* fiber, the text was in Spanish script in an American language, and the painted illustrations were conventional Aztec forms. These pictorial chronicles were made up of single leaves sewn together at the folds in the manner familiar to the missionaries who inspired the production of these books.

The Mexican bindings of the sixteenth century[5] were almost wholly in the European tradition, but always produced with adaptations and compromises necessitated by the remoteness of the metropolis. Hundreds of thousands of books produced in Spain and elsewhere in Roman Catholic Europe were shipped to Mexico and the other colonies in the three centuries of the colonial period, and generally they were "muy bien encuadernados"[6]. Of the books manufactured in the Americas, the vast bulk was covered in a sort of edition binding of vellum, generally with no decoration, and simply folded over the first leaf of the book. Although this custom was dictated by the expense of binder's board and of leather (and the disinclination of Spanish American binders to use covers of wood), it has produced beneficial results for posterity. Combined with the fact that little glue was used, this highly simplified binding contained few attractions for destructive vermin that thrive in these latitudes. Moreover, the very simplicity of these bindings permits them to be opened readily without any serious shock to the spine or the sewing, and rarely does one find broken threads or bands in colonial Spanish American books which have been on shelves where they were subjected only to ordinary use. Generally there is no decoration; if there is a title, it is simply lettered in black ink. Often leather loops were provided in lieu of brass clasps for tighter closing.

From Mexico to Buenos Aires this type of binding prevailed for most books. The primary material existed in abundance everywhere. In the late eighteenth century, when printing came to the La Plata region to stay, it was still in vogue. Father Guillermo Fúrlong, who has probably handled more imprints of this region than any other bibliographer, found this type of binding on the *Catecismo* and the *Novena de la Purísima* of 1781, on the five copies he saw of the *Septenario* of 1781, and other early Buenos Aires imprints of larger size[7].

It would be incorrect to assume that no colonial Spanish American binder showed artistic imagination and skill as a finisher, and there is evidence to the contrary. Srta. Matilde López Serrano, whose total experience with both Spanish and Spanish American bindings is rivalled by that of few, if any, other scholars, has found Mexican books of the sixteenth and seventeenth centuries bound in the *mudéjar* (i.e., hispano-arabic), renaissance, and baroque styles, but most of the bindings are of Spanish origin[8]. Strangely enough—or perhaps not so strange in view of the fantastic ecclesiastical and viceregal bureaucracy—some of the best work of sixteenth century Mexican binders was done on official documents and archives. One of the most remarkable and beautiful examples is the cover on the *Libro General de la Contaduría del Rey Nuestro Señor* for 1588, now in the Archivo General de la Nación in Mexico City. According to Romero de Terreros, it was bound in Mexico. It resembles a portfolio with a flap (highly reminiscent of that on Islamic books!), elaborate gold-stamped flower designs and borders, and embossed ribs stitched with colored silk ribbons in the Italian style. Romero de Terreros states that he has seen similar bindings on the first *Libros de Actas* of the *cabildo* of Mexico City.

The early American printer was frequently a jack of all the book trades. He not only set type and printed, but likely as not he was also a bookbinder and a bookseller. At least all four basic operations in the production and distribution of books were likely to be, and generally were, performed in a single business establishment or religious house. A good example was the struggling José de Pineda Ibarra, the first printer of Guatemala (from 1660 to 1679). It is probable that he operated the tannery in the village of Almolonga mainly for the purpose of supplying raw materials for binding. Antonio de Pineda Ibarra, who printed in Guatemala from 1681 to 1721, produced bulky and (to the age) artistic choir books. In his will there is a pitiful confession that he received eighty pesos from the Indians of San Juan Zacatepeques to make one of these books but failed to do so, for which sin of omission he prayed to God for pardon. During the last war the writer of this article saw a collection of some thirty *libros de canto llano* (plainsong) assembled from cathedrals in the hinterlands of Mexico by a retired SKF salesman. They were seventeenth century books and heavy enough to require bindings in fairly stout cedar or oak boards covered with calf or cowskin. There were large studs to elevate the leather above the level of any sacramental beverage that might have been spilled in the vicinity, and there were iron or brass corners.

We have some little information about conditions under which binders operated in sixteenth century Mexico. Prices of bindings, like nearly all other retail prices, seem to have been regulated carefully. In the *Manuale Sacramentorum* (Mexico, Juan Pablos, 1566), there is a *tasación* of 16 July 1560 from Archbishop Montáfar in which he directs that his secretary, Gaspar Denciso, at whose expense the *Manuale* was printed, might not receive more than three gold pesos for each one, "encuadernado en papelones". The stiff paperback, by the way, was surely a relative luxury by comparison with coverings of animal skins so abundant in a cattle and sheep economy.

We also know something about the equipment of the sixteenth century American binder. When the Seminary of Santa Cruz de Tlalelolco inventoried its bindery in 1584, Father Molina and Father Sahagún reported the following equipment in the celebrated *Códice de Tlaltelolco*: "Una cuchilla grande; dos prensas de madera; un martillo de aplanar, grande, de hierro; dos punzones de hierro; un punzón de golpe; una gubia; dos pares de tijeras pequeñas; tres cosedores; un compás; una caja de cuchillos carniceros; un cepillo de madera; unas tijeras de zapatero; un martillo de hierro, pequeño; tres hierros para pintar la encuadernación; una sierra; una piedra de batir"[10]. The notation of the three single dies is a pitiful symbol of the poverty of the Americas in the basic tools of the finisher's art.

In general the story of binding in the seventeenth century is a continuation of the sixteenth century. The plainsong and choir books are a bit more numerous. Romero de Terreros reports having seen certain private manscripts of special personal significance (e.g., letters patent of nobility, dowry contracts, and charters of pious foundations) bound in velvet, brocade, or damask from this period. The present writer has seen an embroidered cover on a royal land grant covering properties held (or controlled) continuously for almost three centuries by a Zacatecas family, but the binding's ultimate provenance is uncertain. The family had Irish ancestors in Zacatecas as early as 1684, and there is seventeenth century English-made furniture in the homestead that was present as early as 1848.

A few Middle American and Peruvian books of the seventeenth century that survive in contemporary bindings indicate that there were a few more than three dies in some ateliers. Very simple rosettes and flower designs were the main devices, and they appeared in borders, or in circles and squares in the relatively few books on which they appeared. There are rare examples of dies stamped in gold on parchment, and they usually appeared in yellow paint on sheep skin.

In the eighteenth century the art of Padeloup and Derome begins to have some faint reflection in Spanish America. The number of dies begins to proliferate, and their use becomes more imaginative. For the first time we begin to get an abundance of material that might inspire a scholar with the zeal of a Kyriss, and, indeed, precisely such an investigator is needed to provide the full history of binding in eighteenth-century Spanish America. Unfortunately, he cannot confine himself to a small commuting area, but he must travel from Providence to Buenos Aires, from Santiago de Chile to Berlin, to take his rubbings and photographs. A particularly difficult problem will be to identify and distinguish tools and materials which are of American or European origin. In *Some Reflections on the Book Arts in Mexico* L. C. Wroth notes that Mrs. Augustus Loring, the well-known authority on decorated papers, unerringly identified printed end-papers on custom-bound Mexican books of the John Carter Brown Library as being of European, mainly Italian, origin. But how did they come to colonial Mexico, and what perceptive book manufacturer imported them?

A fairly sizeable collection of attractive eighteenth century Mexican bindings might be assembled. Near the top of the list we might record the *Missa gothica* (Angelopolis [*i.e.,*] Puebla de los Angeles], Typis Seminarii Palafoxiana, 1770), certainly an edition binding to judge from the relatively large number of identical copies that exist. There is a flowered border and a circular panel, all in gold. The panel represents a bishop receiving his scapula from an angel and the Virgin. It is difficult not to hazard a guess that the bishop is Palafox de Mendoza himself, for by 1770 his memory endured securely when the power of his implacable enemies, the Jesuits, had been broken. The same scene, by the way, appears on a shield attached to a tower in the frontispiece. An eighteenth century Mexican binding signed by one Francesco Acevedo is recorded in the M. L. Schiff Collection, and there are two illustrations of it there.[11] It is now owned by Major J. R. Abbey. These and other eighteenth century Mexican bindings do not show the meticulously accurate craftsmanship that characterizes the best work in contemporary London, Paris, Madrid, and Italy, but they do impart the pleasing atmosphere of the colonial antique. Indeed one may even trace at times in Mexican bindings of the eighteenth century certain indigenous influences in the interpretation of various European conventions[12].

The heavily predominant use of parchment covers began to give way to sheepskin after the middle of the eighteenth century in both Mexico and Peru, the two oldest printing centers of Spanish America. Good examples of the new trend may be found in the various, *Guías de Forasteros* of Mexico, Guatemala, and Perú. These works appeared in comparatively large editions, and the nature of the market seemed to require more sumptuous bindings than the sturdy old parchment.

European styles, from the lustreless Jansenist to elaborate, occasionally unconsciously caricatured, imitations of German and Italian baroque and rococo styles were cultivated in New Spain and, less frequently, in Peru. An especially interesting phenomenon was the interest of Mexican nuns in making embroidered bindings, often with gold and silver threads on satin, velvet, or linen. Decorations of bone, ivory, and even pearls were not uncommon in the work of these gentle ladies. They even made minature books with embroidered bindings. Don Luís González Obregón of Mexico once had in his library a shelf of such miniatures, some of no more than two centimeters in height.

By the end of the eighteenth century printing and, with it, binding had become indigenous industries throughout Latin America. However, the degree of refinement in binding achieved in Mexico had not yet reached the other "underdeveloped" viceroyalities. Father Fúrlong's notes on the bindings of the earliest Buenos Aires imprints have already been noted. Nevertheless, book production expanded rapidly as an industry in the La Plata region once it took a firm hold there. Speckled and painted edges began to appear, and the *Prevenciones* of 1788 even has a gilt edge that is still quite well preserved. Father Fúrlong describes a *de luxe* copy of this work, perhaps the first *de luxe* binding in Buenos Aires, with a border on both covers and the arms of Spain stamped in the center of each. Incidentally, the aristocratic tradition of armorial binding for libraries of the great families seems not to have taken a firm hold in colonial Spanish America. In the years of independence the sole example of an individual armorial plate that the present writer has found is on the covers of Emperor Maximilian's official documents[13]. The *Prevenciones* was not a cheap book, for it cost six *reales*[14]. The binder in the first Buenos Aires printing house was Antonio López, probably born in 1755 in Ciudad Real in La Mancha. He began his employment there as a binder in 1780.

At present we have only fragmentary notes on early binding in Chile and in New Granada. The rather slippery José Camilo Gallardo, warden of the University of San Felipe in Santiago de Chile and probably the first printer in Chile, told the *cabildo* of Santiago that he could bind their *cedularios* in a communication of 26 May 1810[15]. When printing finally became firmly established in New Granada, Nicolás Caldas acquired one of the two presses that had been shipped to what is now Colombia, and a letter of 16 March 1812 from Tunja reveals a strong preoccupation with the printing press and the binder's press[16]. There is, unquestionably, in the source material for the history of printing in the various countries of Spanish America an abundance of information on the binding processes that went along with printing. Unfortunately, the imprint bibliographers and historians of printing did not see fit to record these data, and the historians of binding, illustration, and bookselling must go back over the sources cited by scholars such as Medina, Fúrlong, Heras and Posada. When they do, they should have a strong sense of indebtedness to these pioneers who have ferreted out the basic sources for the history of the book in Spanish America.

Independence brought comparatively few new ideas in either Latin or Saxon America, and these were less in the arts than in literature. Romantic styles came to Spanish America in belated profusion. In Mexico printers such as Ignacio Cumplido, Rafael Rafael, Marciano Lara, and Mariano Galván Rivera became aware of current traditions in European (especially French) binding and ordered large quantities of tools. Notably popular were tools for "cathedral style" bindings with pointed Gothic windows, and even whole plates were imported. The present writer found such a plate in the papers of a defunct printing house in Monterrey which went bankrupt in the 1920's.

There are some interesting examples of elaborate bindings from the two major colonial possessions remaining to Spain in the nineteenth century, Cuba and the Philippines. Srta. López Serrano found in the library of the Palacio de Oriente in Madrid a copy of Vicente Díaz Comas' *Álbum Regios* (Havana, 1855) offered to Isabel II in rich fabrics and gold, with the crowned seal of Havana and certain elements of the chain of the Order of Carlos II, and a copy of don José María de Laredo's *Poesías al rey don Alfonso XII* (Manila, 1876) with a veneer of Philippine ebony meticulously carved in the manner of ivory, mounted on a cover of silver and a frame or border with a handsome inlay of precious woods and ivory. However, these pieces are spectacular presentation bindings belonging to a timeless (and tasteless) genre. Only too often historians of binding have erroneously treated such special work as period pieces.

Romero de Terreros has properly emphasized the heavy demand for fine binding that developed in Mexico toward the end of the nineteenth century and has continued undiminished through the Revolution and two world wars. He notes such craftsmen as Juan and Jesús Vargas Machuca, Andrés and José del Castillo, A. Delanoé, Celso Jara, Alejandro Freyre, J. Díaz de León, José María Ibarrán, A. Antuñez, and Ignacio Vargas. Several of these binders were skilled finishers, and their work is evident in numerous private libraries of Mexico City, Puebla, and cities of the interior; but in style and inspiration they have generally followed models from Paris and Madrid. Nevertheless, their work is of sufficiently high quality to justify more detailed studies of each binder.

We know much too little about binding in the Spanish-speaking countries of South America in the nineteenth and early twentieth centuries. Thanks to the efforts of Nicolás Chiacchio, engineering librarian of the University of Montevideo, we have the outlines of the recent history of binding in Uruguay[17]. The Escuela de Artes y Oficios of Montevideo, founded in 1880, established a binding atelier as early as 1881 under the direction of Eduardo Como di Candia. While it performed edition binding for the public schools and various government agencies, it was also responsible for some individualized bindings which attracted favorable attention at the expositions in Buenos Aires in 1882 and in Rio de Janeiro in 1884. In 1915 this shop, along with the printing shop of the Escuela, was reorganized as the Imprenta Nacional. Sr. José de Silva, the head of this shop for many years, supervised competent work both in edition binding and in hand bindings. The late Heinrich Rubinstein of Porto Alegre, master of a noble collection of source materials on the southern provinces of Brazil, Paraguay and the La Plata region, owned several bindings executed by de Silva and his pupils which the present writer inspected in 1943. The work was technically perfect, strongly reminiscent of the styles cultivated by the Bozerians and Thouvenin, but worthy of a place on the shelf of any collector of fine modern bindings.

The Universidad de Trabajo of Montevideo has an Escuela de Artes Gráficas in the old quarters of the former Escuela de Artes y Oficios. The professor of binding is González Sorondo, and Srta. Margarita Scavia is his assistant. Together they have directed much competent work by young Uruguayan binders. Chiacchio cites an usually fine *nonato* binding of Hernández' *Martín Fierro* that was done here[18]. Among other Uruguayan binderies which have good finishers are those of the Biblioteca Nacional, directed by Sr. Bordoni, and the Talleres de Don Bosco, supervised by Sr. Gummarus Arnold Uyterhoeven.

In the last few decades Spanish America has benefited substantially from the immigration of well trained European craftsmen. In some instances they have attached themselves to national libraries, but generally they depend on local bibliophiles in a few of the great centers of wealth. For example, Juan Seelig of Montevideo, son and grandson of professional binders in Saxony, has done widely recognized work for private collectors and institutions in the Uruguayan capital. His work is in the traditional German manner, but he has also executed *nonato* bindings for the president of Uruguay and has done numerous restoration jobs on manuscripts and books for the noted Uruguayan collector Octavio C. Assunçao.

Perhaps the one outstanding contemporary binder in Argentina is Julien Leprêtre. A native of Equihen near Boulogne-sur-mer (Pas de Calais), M. Leprêtre served his apprenticeship with Paul Legrand, a well known hand binder of Calais, later studying in the Bernasconi atelier in Paris. In 1936 he was recognized by the jury of the Exposition Nationale with the title of "premier artisan de France", and in 1953 he exhibited in the Galería Witcomb in Buenos Aires. In spite of considerable difficulty in securing materials, M. Leprêtre has done much creditable work for the leading bibliophiles of Buenos Aires, closely following contemporary French styles in finishing, but nevertheless imaginative to some degree, and always in good taste. There is a religious congregation in Buenos Aires known as the "Taller del Divino Rostro" at which young women study binding, but so far no outstanding artists have been produced by this school. Professor Angel Chiesa of Buenos Aires has given instruction in hand binding and artistic leatherwork, but the products of his pupils, as portrayed in illustrations in the *Anales Gráficos*, show little originality[19].

In Chile the best known binder among the bibliophiles of that country is Abraham Contreras, for many years head of the bindery of the Biblioteca Nacional in Santiago and presently operating his own shop in that city. Contreras has executed both original designs (showing clearly the influence of contemporary French binders) and imitations of eighteenth century Spanish styles. The late Santiago Schram, a German binder resident in Santiago, enjoyed an excellent reputation among discriminating Chilean bibliophiles, but the present writer has had no opportunity to examine his work.

In the files of the present writer are the names of a number of Spanish American binders who enjoy good reputations in their own countries, but there has been no opportunity to inspect their work or even to secure photographs. In San Salvador José María

Acosta has received recognition not only by local bookmen but also in the Exposición Ibero-americana of Seville in 1929–30 (diploma of honor and gold medal) and in a national exposition in San Salvador in honor of the third Central American Olympic Games in 1935. Several collectors in Bogotá have recommended highly the work of Encuadernación Biblios, Encuadernación Colombiana, Josué M. Zapata D., Gustavo Gómez, and Daniel Guerrero V. In Caracas Daniel Montenegro M., Arturo Clomont, and Manuel Perez Navas have enjoyed the patronage of local collectors. In Quito Sixto Salguero (care of the Colegio Americano) and the Kilograbado en Cuero have been recommended. The Hermanas Bru, José A. Lázaro and Telmo Bueno Torres are well known Havana hand binders of the present time.

Most edition binding in Spanish America is distinctly inferior both in quality of materials and decorative features. However, at least one exception to this broad statement should be noted. Encuadernación Sauri of Mexico City has done some exceptionally fine edition work for the Fondo de Cultura Económica, one of the leading publishers in the entire Hispanic world. Joaquín García Icazbalceta's *Bibliografía mexicana del siglo XVI* (2d ed., 1954) is bound in half leather (cowhide) with a fully tooled spine. The decoration is tasteful and executed with meticulous care.

The history of binding in Spanish America reveals a spotty tradition, with a few points of excellence, notably in late eighteenth century Mexico and among a few contemporary masters of both American and European origin. Undoubtedly significant bindings, binders, and ateliers have been omitted from these general notes, and they should be supplemented by detailed investigations for each country. The growing strength of Spanish American and Brazilian collectors at European auctions suggests that there may be in the future a much stronger demand for domestic binders of superior quality. At present many of these collectors feel compelled to send their fine books to Paris, Madrid, Barcelona, and, occasionally, London, much in the manner of North American collectors before the turn of the century. It is the volume of their business which will determine whether or not European master craftsmen will be attracted to Latin America and, most important of all, whether or not capable young Americans will appreciate themselves to the craft.

NOTES

1. Nathan van Patten, "Obstetrics in Mexico prior to 1600", *Annals of Medical History*, IV (1932), 203-212, and Laurence C. Wroth, *Some Reflections on the Book Arts in Early Mexico* (Cambridge, Mass., Department of Printing and Graphic Arts, Harvard College Library, 1945).

2. Victor Wolfgang von Hagen, *The Aztec and Maya Papermakers* (New York, J. J. Augustin, 1944), supports this idea.

3. Berthe van Regemorter, "Le codex relié à l'époque néo-Hittite", *Scriptorium*, XII 1958), 177-81 (with illustrations).

4. *Id.*, *Some Early Bindings from Egypt in the Chester Beatty Library* (Dublin, Hodges, Figgis, 1958; "Chester Beatty Monographs", 7).

5. The basic work on the history of Mexican binding (and the best work yet produced on any aspect of the history of Latin American bindings) is Manuel Romero de Terreros y Vinent (marqués de San Francisco), *Encuadernaciones artísticas mexicanas* (second edition; Mexico, 1943; "Biblioteca de la II Feria del Libro y Exposición Nacional del Periodismo"). This second edition was issued under the sponsorship of the Oficina de Bibliotecas, Dirección de Acción Social, Departamento del Distrito Federal. The first edition, entitled *Encuadernaciones artísticas mexicanas, siglos XVI al XIX* (Mexico, 1932), carried the series title "Monografías bibliográficas mevicanas", published by the Secretaría de Relaciones Exteriores. It was abstracted by Rafael Heliodoro Valle in *La Prensa* (Buenos Aires), reference unavailable, and this abstract was reprinted as "Encuadernaciones mejicanas", *Anales gráficos* XXVI (No. 1, Jan., 1935), 10-12. Romero de Terreros printed an English resumé of his work as "Bookbinding in Mexico", *Mexican Art and Life*, No. 7, July, 1939, unpaged (special issue captioned "In the 400th Anniversary of Printing in Mexico").

6. *E. g.*, a shipment of forty boxes of books to Diego Guzmán Navarro Maldonado of Mexico in 1584; *cf.* Francisco Hueso, "Encuadernaciones artísticas españolas", p. 45, in Buenos Aires, Exposición del Libro Español in Buenos Aires, *Doce monografías sobre el libro español* (Buenos Aires, 1933), pp. 43-47.

7. Guillermo Fúrlong Cárdiff, S. J., *Historia y bibliografía de las primeras imprentas rioplatenses, 1700-1850* (Buenos Aires, Editorial Guaranía, 1953-), I, 260-261. This work will consist of several volumes, covering the typographical history of the La Plata region from the beginnings to 1850. Two volumes have appeared thus far.

8. Matilde López Serrano, "En torno a las encuadernaciones artisticas del mundo hispánico", *Boletin de la Dirección General de Archivos y Bibliotecas*, IV (1955), 75-79.

9. José Toribio Medina, *La imprenta en Guatemala (1660-1821)* (Santiago de Chile, Impreso en casa del autor, 1910), pp. xix, xxiii.

10. "One large knife; two wooden presses; one large iron pounding hammer; two iron awls; one awl for driving holes; one gouge; two pairs of small scissors; three stitching tools; a pair of calipers; a box of butcher's knives; one

wood plane; a pair of shoemaker's shears; one small iron hammer; three dies; one saw; one beating stone". See Romero de Terreros, "Bookbinding in Mexico", *loc. cit.*; Heliodoros Valle, "Encuadernaciones mejicanas", *loc. cit.*, p. 10; and Joaquín García Icazbalceta, *Bibliografía mexicana del siglo XVI* (nueva edición por Agustin Millares Carlo, México, Fondo de Cultura Económica, 1954), p. 39. The celebrated *Codice Tlaltelolco* was the property of a Sr. Chavero and was included by García Icazbalceta in the fifth volume of his *Nueva colección de documentos para la historia de México* (México, 1892).

11. Mortimer Leo Schiff, *British and Miscellaneous Signed Bindings in the Mortimer L. Schiff Collection*, by Seymour de Ricci (New York, 1935), No. 77.

12. López Serrano, *loc. cit.*, p. 78.

13. The present writer has also noted the arms of Havana and Manila on the covers of some nineteenth century Cuban and Philippine official documents.

14. Valuable data on the prices of bindings from the printing shop of the Niños Expósitos, the location of the first press in Buenos Aires, may be found in Carlos Heras, *Orígenes de la Imprenta de Niños Expósitos* (La Plata, 1892), and in José Toribio Medina. *Historia y bibliografía de la imprenta en el antiguo virreinato del Rio de la Plata* (La Plata, 1892). Fúrlong quotes extensively from the source material recorded by these two authors.

15. Medina, *Bibliografía de la imprenta en Santiago de Chile desde sus orígenes hasta febrero de 1817* (Santiago de Chile, Impreso en casa del autor, 1891), prints the text of the pertinent letter on p. xviii.

16. Text in Eduardo Posada, *Bibliografía bogotana* (Bogotá, Imprenta de Arboleda y Valencia, 1917-1925; "Biblioteca de historia nacional", xvi, xxxvi).

17. *La encuadernación en el Uruguay* (Montevideo, 1944; ms. in University of Kentucky Library).

18. No-nato = unborn; *nonato* bindings are those in the hide of an unborn pampas calf, with the hair left on, technically a very difficult job.

19. "Algunos trabajos de la clase de encuadernación a cargo del docente señor Chiesa", *Anales Gráficos*, XXVII (Jan. 1936), following p. 35, and "Encuadernación; primero, segundo, tercero y cuarto cursos; desarrollo del Profesor Angel Chiesa", *ibid.*, XXXI (Jan., Feb., Mar. 1940), page without number.

NOTE FOR THIS EDITION

Illustrations of some of
the bindings mentioned in this essay are
in the original article in
Libri, x (1960), 10-22.

PART FOUR

LIBRARY RESOURCES AND THE BOOK TRADE

Resources for Research in Latin-American Literature in Southern Libraries *

Almost two decades ago I published an essay with the same title in *South Atlantic Studies for Sturgis E. Leavitt* (Washington, D.C., The Scarecrow Press, 1953). Much that I had to say at the time is still valid, for the enduring value of collections such as Mexicana at Texas or early material on exploration and discovery of the Americas at Virginia is obvious. Simply for the lack of sources for acquisition, collections of this sort cannot easily be duplicated today. Nor can we readily accept the ambition of the president of a quondam Southern cow-college (now a distinguished university) whose president asked President Harry M. Wriston of Brown "what this-here John Carter Brown liberry" was. President Wriston replied as well as he could, and the rejoinder came quickly: "Well, I'm planning to have the best damned collection of Americana on the east coast at our place, and I don't care if it costs me $10,000 to do it." I would guess that there are 500—1,000 or more items in the JCB which would fetch $10,000 or more each if copies could be found and sent to auction.

On the other hand, libraries which have been wise enough to collect intensively in well defined geographical areas, periods, or genres during the golden bibliographical age of the fifties and sixties now have collections as irreplaceable as those of the Mexican manuscripts and archives in Austin and the early printed books in the McGregor in Charlottesville. The University of Florida's collection of Caribbeana, largely built over the last quarter of a century, is incomparable, and it includes thousands of items which could be

*Revised and rewritten, 1969, for this volume.

acquired today only by photocopy. The same applies to many other libraries which have assumed Farmington Plan responsibilities for Latin American jurisdictions (and supplemented these acquisitions with material ferreted out by perceptive and judicious scholar-specialists working with acquisition librarians). To stay within our defined area of the South, we can mention the collections of Duke on Ecuador, Tulane on Guatemala, Honduras, and El Salvador, Virginia on Venezuela, and Florida on various Caribbean islands and states on the Caribbean littoral.

Another major factor in development of specialized collections, often unique in scope, have been en bloc purchases made possible by the enormous increase in book funds available to research libraries in the fifties and sixties. Many a collection which would have been dispersed by sales catalogues or at auction in the past has been preserved intact to serve the same purposes for which it was intended by its original master. Most of these en bloc acquisitions have been reported in the columns of *College and Research Libraries.*

A third development of major importance has been the possibility of acquiring current Latin American publications on a comprehensive basis, much the same as plans, now operative, for acquisition of the publications of North America and Western European publications comprehensively. Now a decade old, the Latin American Cooperative Acquisitions Program ("LACAP" — described in a book of the same title by M. J. Savary, published by the Hafner Publishing Company in 1968), has brought tens of thousands of valuable Latin Americana into American research libraries in all parts of the country. It is, of course, sponsored by Stechert-Hafner.

There are several weaknesses in the LACAP. First, it must be frankly admitted that the quality of Latin American publications, non-official as well as official, is a cut below that of most comparable things in North America and Western Europe. Second, the LACAP pays little attention to most official publications, a large proportion of which are the most important things published in Hispanic America (including the fields of literature and the arts as well as others). Third, probably most serious, a very large number of Latin American publications are on poor paper, often no better than newsprint, which simply won't be with us a few years from now.

The obvious answer to preservation of this material economically is microform. A partial answer has been found by the Erasmus Press of Lexington, Kentucky, which now has some 4,000 Latin American official documents and non-copyrighted books issued since 1960 on microfiches and microfilm. In 1970 Erasmus plans to bring out 2,000–3,000 titles, and it is probable that coverage will be even greater in 1971 and future years. The Official Gazette Project, sponsored by the Center for Research Libraries in Chicago, should also be noted, even though it is not a resource primarily useful for literary historians. (The Erasmus film is, since a surprisingly large proportion of Latin American literary publications appear as official or quasi-official imprints.) Neither should the Foreign Newspaper Project, also in the Center for Research Libraries, be ignored, for newspapers, especially in Latin America, are often the most important single type of publication for current belletristic literature.

A constructive development of the fifties and sixties is the increased communication between acquisition specialists. Marietta Daniels' study of *The Seminars on the Acquisition of Latin American Library Materials* (Washington, D.C., Pan American Union, 1962), traces the first six years of work for this important organization. It has not only provided a forum for the discussion, but it has also issued reports and surveys which are invaluable for the Latin American specialist. We need only note the surveys of microfilm projects issued by SALALM.

No architect of a research collection can afford to overlook the use of ancillary material. An enormous amount of reprints in microform has become available since the publication of my original essay. For example, my forthcoming book (possibly simultaneous with the present work) on *The Southern Black in Slavery and Freedom, a Bibliography of Books Available in Microform*, contains hundreds of books pertinent to slavery in the West Indies and other parts of the Caribbean area. The Lost Cause Press' ambitious plan to reprint on Microcard everything in Sabin's *Dictionary of Books Relating to America* is not as quixotic as it might have originally seemed. About 2,000 titles are now available, and production is being stepped up constantly. Perhaps most important for the student of the exploration and discovery of the Americas are the Erasmus Press' projects to reproduce European books before 1601 on 35 mm microfilm. Some 5,000 titles of books printed in the fifteenth and sixteenth centuries in Spain, Portugal, France, Italy, Germany, the Low Countries, and Scandinavia are now available, and some 1,500 titles are added each year. Of course, the larger part of this material does not deal with the Americas, and none deals with current Latin American literature. But what kind of a limping program of Latin American studies would we have without access to works such as Waldseemüller, De Bry, or Hakluyt? A final microform project, now only a-borning, is that of General Microfilms of Cambridge, Massachusetts, to reproduce all titles in José Toribio Medina's *Bibliotheca Hispano-Americana* on 35mm microfilm. The titles of microform projects pertinent for the study of Latin American literature might be multiplied considerably, but those mentioned here give a fair sample.

The remainder of this essay will consist of a revision of and commentary on my original study in the Leavitt Festschrift. There will be no documentation, but the reader is referred to Robert B. Downs, *American Library Resources, a Bibliographical Guide, Supplement 1950–1961* (Chicago, American Library Association, 1962), for studies issued up to the date of publication. SALALM publications will also be a useful supplement.

In 1938 Downs could mention only Texas as an outstanding depository of Latin American literature in his *Resources of Southern Libraries.* Of the University of North Carolina at Chapel Hill he could state authoritatively, as its librarian, that it contained "approximately only 300 volumes" in this field. It would be hazardous to estimate less than a hundred times as many today, possibly even more. Duke (then barely a decade from the chrysalis of old Trinity College, Virginia, Vanderbilt [i.e., present Joint University Library]), and Tulane barely seemed worth mention. Florida State University didn't even exist as a research collection, and places such as Louisiana State, Florida, Oklahoma, Miami at Coral Gables, and Alabama—all fairly strong today in Latin Americana— could hardly claim status as research libraries. By the same token, in 1953, when my original essay was written, institutions such as Murray State University, East Tennessee State University, and East Carolina University barely contained enough volumes in all to meet Southern Association standards. Today these libraries are probably better off in our field than were the leading universities of 1938.

It is highly significant that Southern research libraries recognized their limitations in the 1930s and attempted to divide fields of concentration among themselves. It is likely that these efforts had some influence on the development of the Farmington Plan, the Scandia Plan in Scandinavia, and a similar agreement among West German research libraries. In the forties there was an agreement between Duke University, Tulane University, and the University of North Carolina at Chapel Hill under which the first collected material relative to Bolivia (still its Farmington Plan responsibility, *supra*), Brazil, Colombia, Ecuador, and Peru; the second, Central America, Mexico, and Caribbean areas; and the third, most other South American countries. Foundations (Rockefeller and Carnegie) thought well enough of the idea to support it in effective terms.

For obvious reasons, Texas had long specialized in Mexican culture, and the collections in Austin are unrivalled, even in Mexico. When Florida State (the old Women's College) emerged as a university, it wisely chose a similar course by selecting Peru as its field of specialization. The museum of Peruvian art and artifacts is well supported by handsome book collections. Virginia, through the "come-hither" genius of the late John Cooke Wyllie, could attract a gift of $5,000 from the Creole Petroleum Corporation, to establish a collection of Venezolana in Charlottesville which is maintained currently by Virginia's commitment to the Farmington Plan in this area. A special case should be noted in a regional collection in one of the newest universities south of Washington, the University of Puerto Rico Library in Rio Piedras. As early as the mid-thirties Puerto Rico had a collection of Borincana, heavily dependent on the private library of the late Antonio S. Pedreira, which was even then as strong, qualitatively, as any state collection in a North American state university library. Today it is incomparable in its field.

In some instances personal contacts have been responsible for modest Latin American area collections. Thus a visit of the late Frank L. McVey, president of the University of Kentucky in the twenties and thirties, to Venezuela, is still responsible for a steady flow of material to this institution. The long residence in Puerto Rico of a teacher in the same institution has been responsible for a basic collection in this field. Personal visits by members of the University of Tennessee's Department of Romance Languages to Costa Rica, Colombia, and Ecuador resulted in the same thing for that institution.

In the early period Latin American history and literature are inseparable; and for the age of exploration, conquest, and colonization the University of Virginia's noble McGregor Library beggars description and rivals the holdings of the Lenox, the John Carter Brown, and the William L. Clements Libraries. It has original editions of Hakluyt, Peter Martyr, the Inca Garcilasso, Purchas, De Bry, Las Casas, Waldseemüller, and related monuments. The reference works ancillary to these valuable books are themselves quite complete, containing such collections as Navarrete's calendars of the Archives of the Indies, the bibliographies of Medina, Icazbalceta, and similar materials. The wealth of the McGregor may be further illustrated by odd philological works printed in Mexico in the sixteenth century, the *Araucana* of 1592, the Esquemelings of 1678 and 1684/84, Fernández' *Historia del Peru* of 1571, the Herrera of 1601, the Castañeda of 1582, the Cieza de León of 1553 and 1560, the Gómaras of 1552/53 and 1578, the Oviedos of 1535 and 1557, and dozens of other similar titles that fetch high prices whenever they appear on the antiquarian market. In addition to the Venezuelan collection in Charlottesville, there are also strong Panamanian, Mexican, and Peruvian materials, although they run to history and politics more than to literature.

Consistent with the Duke University Library's general strength as one of the South's largest and best libraries, it is outstanding in Latin American studies in general, and it has collections of considerable distinction in the literature and history of several countries. One of the foundation stones of Duke's collection is the Peruvian material originally assembled by Francisco Pérez, a private library that was especially strong in books and manuscripts from the colonial period. In 1940 the Rockefeller Foundation made a grant to Duke, the University of North Carolina, and Tulane to support the cooperative acquisition project to which reference has already been made. Duke used its $25,000 for government documents (of which it has one of the most distinguished collections in existence), history, and literature; and at the same time the library supplemented Rockefeller funds with several thousand dollars for additional purchases, a gesture that hardly any other Southern library could afford to make. In the course of this program 7,624 volumes were received. A subsequent grant made in 1947 by the Carnegie Corporation (for personnel as well as books) added further to the resources of Duke, North Carolina, and Tulane in their respective fields. Duke's Brazilian collections have always been unusually strong, and the excellent files of Brazilian academy and learned society publications are as significant resources for the study of Brazilian literature and folklore as for history. Although the Philippine Islands are beyond the scope of this essay, they may properly be discussed with the former colonies of Spain; and here again Duke is usually strong, having the 5,000-item collection of the late James A. Robertson's Filipiniana acquired in 1940. The Robertson collection is primarily historical and political, but it does include literature. A final important factor in the development of Duke's Latin-American collections has been the fact that the *Hispanic-American Historical Review* has been published by the Duke University Press since 1926. Just as *Books Abroad* has had a basic influence in building a good collection of Latin American poetry at the University of Oklahoma, so has the *Hispanic-American Historical Review* had a similiar effect in its own field at Duke. In summary it may be said that Duke's collections in Latin-American literature and good files of literary periodicals represent solid foundation material in the fields of criticism, anthologies, poetry, modern prose fiction, bibliography, biography, and periodicals.

Sturgis Leavitt has provided the best available description of holdings in Spanish and Latin-American literature in the University of North Carolina Library. Under the Rockefeller grant 12,687 volumes of history and literature pertaining to the countries in North Carolina's sphere were added to the library. In addition to the geographical specialization as outlined under the terms of the original Rockefeller grant, North Carolina was unrestricted in bibliography and folklore and has been quite successful in building its resources in these fields. North Carolina has some particularly fine runs of Argentine and Chilean literary periodicals and sets of major Latin-American authors, as well as a representative selection of individual works of literary importance. One important addition is worthy of special mention, a gift containing a file of *La Presna* (Buenos Aires), 1905 to date, with some gaps in 1932.

The preëminence of Texas in the field of Latin American literature is common knowledge, and the holdings of the great library in Austin probably excel those of all the rest in this field. The Latin American Collection at Texas also includes thousands of other works of a literary nature but classified as bibliography, religion, and history. Texas is quite adequate for research in Spanish American literature in general, and it is almost fabulously rich in Mexicana, historical and literary. A catalog of the remarkable manuscript collection (predominantly Mexican) was issued over three decades ago. Texas is committed to an active and aggressive acquisition program, and it is constantly adding such gems as the Hernández y Dávalos documents (1700-1840) or the Sánchez Navarro papers (1658-1895). Texas' wealth in Mexican literature may be illustrated by a single item (of many) in its manuscript collection, four volumes which include thirty *entremeses* and *comedias* given in Mexico around 1835 and some twenty other works, including a collection of poetry, a poem of Guridi y Alcocer, and two versions of *La monja alférez*. The intimate relationship of historical literature and belles letters, especially in the colonial period, is obvious at once from an examination of such poems in the Texas collection as those on the death of a viceroy or on a religious or academic celebration. Texas' bibliographical collection has few rivals in North America outside of the Library of Congress; and it includes, *inter alia*, a collection of some two hundred volumes by José Toribio Medina. The University of Florida owns a comparable collection of Medina from the library of Maury Bromsen. Texas' materials from the period of conquest and colonization rival Virginia's, and it even owns the original manuscript of Cortés' *Carta de relación* of 15 October 1524. In this brief essay it can only be said that Texas' riches in Latin-American and especially Mexican literature reveal the same quality in general as these few examples indicate and that the more recent periods are as well represented as the older periods.

The special strength of the Tulane University Latin-American collection lies in Middle America; and the foundation grants have been supplemented by book purchasing expeditions undertaken in the thirties by faculty members in this area. The value of the Tulane collection in Middle American literature is greatly enhanced by the related collections in the Middle American Research Institute, especially in such ancillary fields as anthropology, folklore, linguistics, and travel literature. In the field of Latin American linguistics Tulane has few rivals in the entire country. Virtually all standard works in the field of American Spanish are available at Tulane; and the Middle American Institute collection contains numerous Indian language dictionaries and grammars, some in manuscript. The Tulane Library has complete sets of a number of Latin-American periodicals found in few other collections, e.g., *Amauta, Revista America, Azul, Revista Bimestra Cubana, Sur, Nosotros,* and *Repertorio Americano.* In the field of Brazilian literature Tulane has a rather complete collection of contemporary novels and a good selection of Brazilian poets and short story writers.

The Joint University Library in Nashville also has substantial holdings in Brazilian literature, history, and culture. Serious students of Brazil will neglect this collection at their own peril.

The rapid growth of three of Florida's universities since the end of the war has been a powerful stimulus to the development of Latin-American collections at Gainesville, Coral Gables, and Tallahassee. The University of Florida's very considerable book funds have enabled its library to acquire significant early works (e.g., the Inca and Las Casas) which may permit it ultimately to approach Virginia and Texas in the field. Although Florida's collections are still spotty as far as the nineteenth century is concerned, some notion of the vigor of the current acquisition policy may be gained from the fact that most of the articles indexed in the *Handbook of Latin American Studies* and the *Revista Interamericana de Bibli-*

ografía are available in current periodicals in the Florida list. The special emphasis on the Caribbean area is also proving to be especially fruitful, but at the same time every effort is being made to build sound general collections in the literature of other Latin-American countries. At Florida State University a similar program is enjoying considerable success, although that institution's very recent emergence as a university and consequent lack of background material has been a genuine challenge to the library in building its collections in all fields. Like the two other major institutions in Florida, the University of Miami has also been blest with abundant book funds in recent years. Its collection of contemporary Spanish-American poetry is outstanding, and it has a representative list of current literary periodicals as well as bibliographies, biographical dictionaries, and other reference works.

Some three decades ago Louisiana State University enjoyed a boom comparable to the one now under way in Florida's universities; and, as far as library resources are concerned, it has maintained its rate of development. At the University of Alabama there has been a strong development of Latin-American holdings since the war, but Alabama still has much ground to cover and has developed no specialty. The T. P. Thompson Collections at Tuscaloosa contains materials bearing on Spanish Louisiana which rival (but do not equal) the collections at Tulane in some respects. The University of Oklahoma Library has solid collections of contemporary literature, a good current periodical list, and the basic bibliographical tools. Much the same thing is true at the University of Kentucky. This institution enjoyed remarkable success in recent years in soliciting presentation copies from contemporary Latin-American authors, and some 2,000 volumes have been added in this manner. It has been discovered at Lexington that the worst thing that can happen to a carefully phrased, courteous letter of solicitation is an equally courteous reference to a bookseller. The great majority of Latin-American authors are flattered and pleased to deposit presentation copies (sometimes in duplicate and triplicate—a real problem of disposition brought on by aggressive acquisition policies!).

However sketchy this survey has been, certain important conclusions on policy, cooperation, and lines for future development may be drawn from it. It has already been made abundantly clear that the programs of specialization are paying dividends. Even the truly great libraries such as Texas and Duke, blest over the years with twice the book funds that most other institutions in the region enjoy, cannot hope to cover all of Latin America comprehensively. The success of Texas in becoming the world's greatest depository of Mexican history and literature and in building outstanding general collections for other Latin-American countries is an instructive example of effective library planning. No great damage is done by some duplication such as specialization in Peru at both Duke and Florida State, in Brazil at both Duke and the Joint University Library, or in Venezuela at both North Carolina and Virginia. Two depositories are in order to insure comprehensive coverage of ephemera, limited editions, minor serials, and other publications that are likely to escape even the most meticulous acquisition librarian. However, additional depositories would be waste of effort, money, and space.

The Southern research libraries have learned the necessity of cooperation among themselves and the futility of competition either within the region or with the great libraries in the East and the Middle West. They may, however, select a few fields in which they can properly attain preëminence; and the whole broad Latin-American field, properly divided among the institutions in the region, is one that comes to mind at once. This means that the Southern institutions of higher learning must realize the full burden of the responsibility not only by mere piling up of books but also by publication programs. Excellent examples may be found in Florida's School of Inter-American Studies, originally under the stimulating leadership of Curtis Wilgus, the Hispanic American Institute at the University of Miami, and the significant gesture by the University of Florida in assuming responsibility for the publication of the *Handbook of Latin American Studies.*

In order to promote the development of Latin-American collections we need more bibliographical activity on all fronts. (Or perhaps in order to encourage the development of Latin-American bibliography we need to develop better book collections.) The *Union List of Latin American Newspapers in Libraries in the United States,* compiled by the Columbus Memorial Library of the

Pan American Union, is a fine example of a project that is basically useful to scholarship and also will stimulate the intelligent development of library collections. As manuscript collections grow, lists such as Castañeda and Dabbs and Tilley and Goodwin will be needed. The useful set of guides to official publications of the other American republics issued by the Library of Congress will need periodic revision every decade or so. At present we are urgently in need of a new edition of the little guide to Latin-American exchanges issued by the American Library Association a decade ago. We need a comprehensive list of masters' essays and doctoral theses on all aspects of Latin America much like the list of theses on Southern literary culture by Cantrell and Patrick. This list of projects could be extended over several pages, but without the imagination and the active direction of a few leaders in strategic positions, they will remain pipe dreams of librarians who want their collections to grow and become increasingly useful but who lack the training to develop specific fields. Libraries and bibliographical projects need the strong hand of a competent administrator, but none will thrive without the benefit of the vision, energy, and genius of leaders like Sturgis Leavitt.

The Antiquarian Book Trade
In Spain[*]

There is no adequate history of the book trade in Spain. Oliva's El librero español (1930) and Vindel's El librero español (1934) contain some historical information. Palau y Dulcet's Memorias de un librero catalan 1867–1935 (1935) has many intimate notes on the experiences of a master bibliographer and highly respected dealer in the second half of the past century. Dr. Ettinghausen's Rare Books and Royal Collectors (1966) provides some informative notes on sources of manuscripts, private archives, and rare printed books in Spain and Portugal. However his bibliographical carpetbagging on the Peninsula is more a part of the history of the English book trade than of that of the Spanish.

The origins of the organized book trade in the Peninsula go back to the latter half of the fifteenth century, beginning in Valencia in 1475 when Jakob Vizlant of Ravensburg had some fifteen books printed by German printers (Lambert Palmart of Cologne, Johannes de Salsburga, and Paulus Hurus). The fact that a large proportion of the early printers in Spain were natives of the Germanies paved the way for close association with the book trade of countries to the north. The authorities in Spain during this period recognized clearly the need for dissemination of knowledge, and a law of 1480 provides that "no duties whatsoever shall be paid for the importation of foreign books into these kingdoms, in order that by them men may become learned" (Novisima recopilación

*Reprinted with permission of the publisher from The 1969 AB Bookman's Yearbook, Part II, pp. 29-31.

de leyes de España, lib. viii, tit. xv, ley 1). But this intelligent legislation was virtually cancelled by a statute of 8 July 1502 which prohibited publication or sale of any book except after rigorous censorship. Another equally repressive edict was the cédula of Charles V in September 1543 virtually forbidding printing, importation and sale in the Indies of books dealing with profane subjects. Although this ruling was aimed primarily at the libros de caballerías, Irving Leonard has shown in Books of the Brave (1949) and elsewhere that it had little or no effect.

In the colonial period the metropolis looked upon the American vice-royalties as a major market for books as well as for other exports. The well-nigh airtight contract between Jaun Pablos and Juan Cromberger dated 12 June 1539 put the former in the position of being a sales agent for Cromberger as well as the operator of his press in Mexico City. Most colonial printers were also booksellers, but there is evidence of one Andrés Martín, who was keeping a tienda de libros in Mexico City in 1541 and was not a printer. In the colonies, and probably also in the metropolis, some social opprobrium was attached to the profession of bookselling, since in 1573 Viceroy Enriquez referred to it as an oficio bajo.

The Spanish book trade, already in a precarious situation at the end of the Napoleonic wars, suffered even more in the nineteenth century with the loss of the American colonies; but after the unhappy experience of the war of 1898 with the United States of America, special efforts were made to regain the Spanish American book market. Nevertheless, we have such depressing statistics as those from Cuba in 1918/19, according to which only five kilograms of books were imported from Spain, 22,661 kilograms in the Spanish language from the U.S.A. On the other hand, Colombia was importing 60 per cent of her foreign books from Spain, 20 per cent from the U.S.A. England, France, and Germany also competed for the Latin American book market. In the 1920s Latin America as a whole spent some $15,000,000 a year for foreign books, of which less than a million was for books printed in Spain. In the 1950s and 1960s the balance is shifting somewhat in favor of Spain. One significant point to remember in this connection is that the high rate of illiteracy in Spain itself has always militated against large editions of the ordinary book.

Returning to the sixteenth century, it is important to remember that many great fortunes were established with the influx of bullion from the New World and that even moderately bibliophilic gentry were likely to assemble important collections of books and manuscripts. Many of these collections stayed in family hands for centuries. Some began to deteriorate in the last century, and the process was accelerated in the 1930s with the Civil War. The decline of family fortunes in the Peninsula was noted by French dealers as early as the middle of the last century. French publishers and retailers (e.g., Baillière and Monier) had begun to establish themselves in the Peninsula (mainly in the capitals, but also in Barcelona and Porto) soon after the end of the Napoleonic wars. Word soon got to antiquarian dealers about the rich family libraries and private archives, and from France the news spread to England, the Germanies, and even to New England. George Ticknor gave the Peninsula a taste of bibliological carpetbagging long before his Boston confrères began to make their millions in the prostrate South. In our own day Dr. Ettinghausen has ferreted out some remarkable collections in Spain and Portugal for the collectors of France, England, and the U.S.A. His own account in Rare Books and Royal Collectors is composed in a sort of dignified Dibdenian or Powellian style.

Much the same story has been repeated in the influential ecclesiastical jurisdictions. In the sixteenth and seventeenth centuries the regular clergy of all orders sent back untold thousands of books and manuscripts not only from the Americas, but also from the Levant, Africa, and Asia. A few lucky souls managed to return to the metropolis and spend their declining years studying and editing their collectanea, ultimately to go to some episcopal or cathedral collections. And many of the military and civil officials who have served abroad sent the books and manuscripts they had liberated to the same depositories. In the mid-twentieth century a cathedral collection such as that of Zaragoza was rich enough to incite the baser motives of adventurers who were only on the periphery of the antiquarian trade. What slight payment that might have been made would be allegedly dedicated to building and repair funds. This sordid story can be read in fragmentary reportage in the late fall 1964 issues of AB and LJ.

The whole truth about this incident may or may not come out in full detail. But there will be others like it in the future. The Miscatonic University Library acquired recently a remarkable collection of notarial documents of the twelfth through the early seventeenth centuries, many of which bore the partially erased stamps of the Archivo Municipal de Carabobo. And a fine autograph of Charles V on a royal cédula forbidding cockroach racing in Camargo is in the Memorial Library at Old Siwash. The poverty of Hispanic countries, the relatively underdeveloped concept of a categorical imperative and, perhaps most compelling, the substandard salaries of ecclesiastical and civil authorities alike have created this situation.

A related problem in Spain centers around the outrageous customs and export regulations. On several occasions owners of collections which are duplicated in Spanish libraries (probably three or more times—a reliable Spanish union catalogue would tell the story) have been denied an export license. This is pure nonsense in a country so desperately in need of valuta, and it is insulting to competent bibliographers who flourish in Spain. The Arturo Sedó Cervantes Collection which the University of Wisconsin attempted to purchase is an egregious example of this sort of official tomfoolery. Minor pieces can be brought out of Spain easily in most cases. The University of Kentucky Library has a handsome early sixteenth century antiphonal which was dumped on top of camping equipment in a Volkswagen station wagon "to keep the tent and blankets from blowing off the car". The aduanero waved the vehicle over the border for a pack of Camels. In most countries this side of Prag the omnipresent APO is by far the simplest channel for shipment of books from abroad (and at domestic rates).

These aspects of the Spanish antiquarian book trade are more germane to the story of the business in North America, England, and northwestern Europe than to Spain. In Spain proper the early history of the book trade is not much different from the story in Italy, France, and the Germanies, but much scaled down. Despite the great fortunes accumulated in the sixteenth and seventeenth centuries, Spain produced only a royal collector in Philip II, no private collectors on the order of a Fugger, a De Thou, a Mazarin, or a Cotton. Books were brought together haphazardly in most cases, not collected. There was no bibliophilic market for Spanish dealers, and there is no instance of a dealer with the vision of a George Thomason. The book auction did not take root until quite late. Spanish auctions are still relatively unimportant, although the very word for auction, subasta (from sub hasta, "under the spear") reflects the antiquity of the concept in general in Spain.

Much as the earlier printers were itinerant, so too were many of the early booksellers. Thus they were not in a position to maintain large stocks. Luis Batlle y Prats, archivist of the Ayuntamiento of Gerona, has excavated some significant documents on these points. In his "Notas para la biografía del impresor Pedro Malo y para la historia de la imprenta en Gerona," (Biblioteconomía [Barcelona], v. IV, 1947, no. 13, p. 5), he tells the curious story of the efforts of the printer Pedro Malo, active in Barcelona since 1565, to set up a printing establishment (and, surely, the inevitable retail book shop) in Gerona in 1577. In the same journal, v. XVIII, 1960, p. 76-7, Batlle y Prats tells how "un librero barcelonés en las Ferias de Gerona de 1699", one Juan Piferrer, Llibreterius civis Barcinone, sought special privileges to peddle his wares in Gerona. His petition was endorsed by the Gerundene bookseller Francisco Oliva, a circumstance which suggests a previous agreement between the two. In any event, Piferrer's stock could have been no more bulky than what a couple of mules could transport—say, roughly the equivalent of three or four black steamer trunks carried by our metropolitan dealers to libraries in the North American bibliological boondocks in the twentieth century.

Into our own times the hole-in-the-wall bookshop with relatively small stocks has been the order of the day in Spain, Portugal, and Latin America. It is almost possible to count on the fingers of two hands the dealers who have stocks that are qualitatively and quantitatively equivalent to those of, say, José Porter in Barcelona or Hesperia in Zaragoza. Even fewer are those whose catalogues reflect a bibliographical diligence comparable to that of these two dealers (again, as examples). Even in the famed Calle de los Libreros in Madrid the small shop with mediocre stocks is the rule rather than the exception. Indeed, in the Callejón near the Plaza del Sol a relatively small shop held, at least up until a few years ago, the bibelot entitled El Rezo del Santo Rosario for which Don Francisco Vindel so passionately claimed primacy among the incunabula of North America. Encased within boxes, much as a hair from the beard of the Prophet or one of Jeff Davis' whiskers in the University of the Confederacy, it was described as "muy, muy raro—rarissimo! "—then repacked and securely locked in the drawer of a wooden desk. If it could be established as the first American imprint, only a congressional appropriation would be sufficient to buy it.

Geographically the Spanish book trade centers in Madrid (specifically in the Calle de los Libreros) and Barcelona. Still it is somewhat more widely spread out, geographically, than the French or even the Italian trade, about the same as in Britain. There are antiquarian shops worth visiting in Valencia, Gerona, Valladolid, Zaragoza, Majorca, Bilbao, Sevilla, Cadiz, and elsewhere. One United States national has even rented a casilla postal in a tiny fishing village on the Costa Brava, and he writes that he is able to earn enough to survive on pulpos and white wine.

In 1917 a Cámara Oficial del Libro was founded in Barcelona, in 1922 an organization of the same name in Madrid. Since the Civil War the organization has been defined in Falangista terms, but it has essentially the same functions and purposes. In 1929 a vocational school for booksellers was established in Madrid, and in 1931 an Asociación Nacional de Amigos del Libro was formed. All of these activities directed toward the modernization of the Spanish book trade, both antiquarian and retail, were redefined in the language of the corporate state after 1939. The forms and functions, not unlike those of similar agencies in other western European countries, have not been substantially changed.

The future of the antiquarian book trade in Spain is nebulous. There will always be inspired and scholarly antiquarians such as Vindel and Porter, collectors with the zeal and bird-dog accuracy of an Arturo Sedó, indefatigable bibliographers of the calibre of Simón Diaz. Whether they will proliferate is a matter of conjecture.

There will be treasure troves of family collections which may stay on the market as long as those of Sir Thomas Phillipps. It cannot be predicted whether they will come under the spear (let's use the medieval term!) in Spain or in Northern Europe. If those who shape Spanish export regulations do not show a bit more common sense, the answer is Northern Europe.

Some aspects of the leyenda negra about Spain persist today. To be sure, the Peninsula is less fortunate than North America or northwestern Europe from the standpoint of economic development. Yet the best traditions of Hispanic culture are the same as those of northwestern Europe. Whatever rascality that may have transpired in the Zaragoza Cathedral, if any, was little more iniquitous than the vandalism of the choir boys at Lincoln who amused themselves by clipping initials from manuscripts while waiting their turn to sing. The proud U.S. Customs has known its scandals. And in the hinterlands of the U.S.A. the antiquarian book trade is generally more primitive than it is in Zaragoza, Valladolid, Gerona, or Bilbao.

Spain will probably never be a major center of the antiquarian book trade. But this great country has gradually recovered from the disastrous politics of 1492, the Peninsular Wars, the Carlist Wars, and the Civil War. It is likely that the Spanish book trade, both retail and antiquarian, will develop in stature and international prestige in the coming decades.